VOICES OF
BLACK
AMERICA

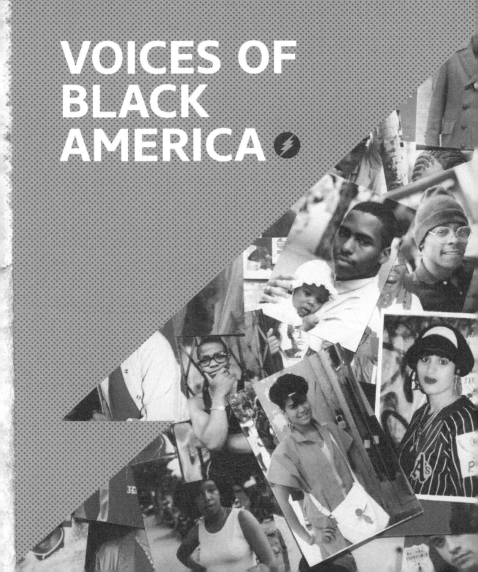

VOICES OF
BLACK
AMERICA

MLK, JR. TO JAY Z

LIGHTNING
GUIDES

ISBN Print 978-1-942411-37-6
eBook 978-1-942411-38-3

"Never underestimate the power of dreams and the influence of the human spirit. We are all the same in this notion: The potential for greatness lives within each of us."

—WILMA RUDOLPH, THREE-TIME OLYMPIC GOLD MEDALIST

Against the backdrop of one of the darkest moments in American history, the voices of the ongoing Civil Rights Movement offer a scintillating and excoriating perspective into the dream and struggle that is America. Every day we are reminded that the battle is not yet won, that all lives matter, and we realize that in the ability to exercise our most fundamental human right, our right to free speech and uplifted voices, lies our greatest opportunity for victory. Poets and politicians. Actors and abolitionists. Writers and dreamers and preachers and everyday heroes. These are the voices that shape America.

CONTENTS

INTRODUCTION

The history of African American people in America has been marked by hard-earned victories for, and crushing blows to, the prosperity of an entire race. From the West Africans who found themselves ensnared by slavers in the 17th century, to the trials, tribulations, and eventual freedoms brought by the Civil War; from the fight for civil rights in the 20th century, to the modern media outlets that appear caught unawares by racial tensions in small towns—there is no straightforward narrative of the African-American experience that leads intuitively from one step to the next.

When we listen to the voices of Black America, we hear individual people, each one with a distinct perspective on their time and place. Though there may be myriad differences between them, all those voices make a unique contribution to the black experience. Some, like Malcolm X, Martin Luther King Jr., and Angela Davis, have made it into the history books as champions of social justice and Black American culture in all its forms. But millions of other people have struggled in their own ways with being black in America, and their stories, too, are essential parts of the whole.

Here is one account of how black activism has changed over the years, from the Civil Rights movement to #blacklivesmatter. No one can tell the full story, with all its courage, triumph, survival, and bittersweet struggle. But we can give context to some of the voices that rise above. The individuals featured here—and too many more to fit within these pages—have left an indelible imprint on the world.

FIRST, A FEW FACTS

MICHAEL JACKSON'S
1982 ALBUM
THRILLER
IS THE BEST-SELLING ALBUM IN HISTORY

MALCOLM X
WAS ASSASSINATED ON
FEBRUARY 21, 1965

DECEMBER 1, 1955
ROSA PARKS
was arrested for
NOT GIVING UP
HER SEAT
on the
BUS

BARACK OBAMA
BECAME THE FIRST
BLACK
PRESIDENT
★★ *of the* ★★
UNITED
STATES
★★ *in* ★★
2008

in
1992
MAE JEMISON
BECAME THE FIRST
BLACK
FEMALE
ASTRONAUT

Who was the first African American to be awarded the Nobel Prize? Political scientist and UN diplomat Ralph Bunche was awarded the Nobel Peace Prize in 1950 for his work moderating the 1949 armistice in the Arab-Israeli conflict, becoming the first African American to be honored with the prestigious prize. Bunche continued his UN service into the 1960s, mediating conflict in the Congo, Yemen, Kashmir, and Cyprus. More than four decades later, in 1993, novelist Toni Morrison became the first African American woman to receive the Nobel Prize, which she was awarded in literature.

What is the Civil Rights Act of 1964?
 A landmark piece of Civil Rights legislation, the Civil Rights Act of 1964 outlawed segregation in all public places and most private businesses, and banned employment discrimination on the basis of race, color, sex, religion, or national origin. President John F. Kennedy introduced the bill in 1963, and Lyndon B. Johnson signed the bill into law on July 2, 1964.

How many African Americans have served on the United States Senate?
Nine, though only seven have been popularly elected (United States senators were appointed by state legislators until 1913). In 1870, the Mississippi State Legislator appointed Hiram Revels to fill a senate seat that had been vacant since the Civil War, making him the first African American to serve on the

United States Senate. It wasn't until 1966 that Edward Brooke became the first African American popularly elected to the senate. Brooke has been followed by six other African American senators, including Barack Obama.

Who founded Motown Records?

Berry Gordy, Jr. founded Motown Records in January 1959. At the urging of his friend William "Smokey" Robinson, Gordy took an $800 loan from his family and set up shop in a house on Detroit's West Grand Boulevard. The Miracles' "Shop Around", written by Smokey Robinson, became Motown Record's first smash hit in 1960, and the Marvelettes' "Please Mr. Postman" became the label's first #1 song in 1961.

What sparked the #BlackLivesMatter movement?

In February 2012, George Zimmerman shot and killed unarmed seventeen-year-old Trayvon Martin in Stanford, Florida. When Zimmerman was acquitted of Martin's murder in July 2014, the hashtag #BlackLivesMatter was coined and quickly sparked a movement that spread across the US and the world. The movement gained momentum after the police shooting of Michael Brown in Ferguson, Missouri and the chokehold death of Eric Garner at the hands of a plainclothes police officer in Staten Island, New York, both in 2014, and after the death of Freddie Gray while in police custody in Baltimore in 2015.

SHAPING MANY MOVEMENTS

THE LIFEBLOOD OF AFRICAN-AMERICAN HISTORY IN THE UNITED STATES

The Black Power movement was a direct outgrowth of the Civil Rights movement in the late 1960s. Until then, the majority of African Americans had perceived Martin Luther King Jr.'s nonviolent resistance as the prime method for viable social, political, and economic change in the United States. Many began to associate the emergence of the Black Power movement with violence and separatism. However, in 1968, Stokely Carmichael of the Student Nonviolent

Overhead view of the massive crowd assembled on the Mall in Washington DC, August 28, 1963. It was at this rally that Martin Luther King Jr. delivered his "I Have a Dream" speech.

Coordinating Committee (SNCC) defined Black Power "as the ability of black people to politically get together and organize themselves so that they can speak from a position of strength rather than a position of weakness." Malcolm X's contention that integration into white America was not the best option for African Americans, coupled with psychiatrist and writer Frantz Fanon's visceral analysis of the effects of colonization, *The Wretched of the Earth*, paved the way for many prominent organizations. These groups included the Black Panther Party, the Republic of New Africa, the League of Revolutionary Black Workers, and the Revolutionary Action movement.

Black Power supporters were inspired by the struggles for independence on the continent of Africa. Fueled by Malcolm X's assassination in 1965, and the Watts riots in Los Angeles the same year, the Black Power movement was in full force by 1968. One of the most visible differences between the Civil Rights movement and the Black Power movement was that while King's Civil Rights movement was Christian-themed and Southern-based, the Black Power movement ran the gamut of political and religious perspectives as its organizations spread throughout the United States.

The Black Power movement celebrated Marcus Garvey's Black Nationalism chant of the Harlem Renaissance (1915–1930), while combining political activism with a radical shift in consciousness-raising for African Americans. In this climate of consciousness, African Americans began calling themselves black instead of Negro. Black student activists from Cornell University to the University of California–Berkeley began establishing black student unions and demanding the establishment of black studies programs with black faculty. With sparse African and African-American history taught in classrooms, African-American students wanted access to their heritage, taught by instructors who looked like them. Years before this movement, Carter G. Woodson, historian and Founder of *The Journal of Negro History*, neatly summed up what he foresaw as the future of African-American studies, saying, "The Negro knows practically nothing of his history and his 'friends' are not permitting him to learn it. And if a race has no history, if it has no worthwhile tradition, it becomes a negligible factor in the thought of the world, and it stands in danger of extermination."

Across campuses and in the streets, the slogan "Black is Beautiful," coupled with Afros and dashikis, were the visible indicators of Black Power consciousness. The Black Power movement was firmly rooted in rich traditions of black protest. As a whole, the movement was influential in literature, songs, theater, visual arts, and grassroots African-American community organizations.

Following the Black Arts Movement, hip-hop emerged as a cultural expression

BLACK ARTS

The Black Arts Movement, set in motion by Amiri Baraka (above) in 1965, was a direct result of Black Power consciousness. The Black Arts Movement promoted black cultural and artistic spaces based in predominantely African-American communities.

....

✳ **"Black is Beautiful,"** Afros, and dashikis were visible indicators of Black Power consciousness.

....

of African-American music and art comprising four main elements: emceeing, DJing, graffiti, and break-dancing. Rap is a musical form originating in hip-hop culture, which began in the 1970s with Jamaican DJ Kool Herc in the Bronx, New York. Herc combined DJing with reciting rhymes over instrumentals. At first, hip-hop was entertainment for a community looking around at its environment and seeing only devastated Bronx city streets, which resembled a war zone of empty lots and dilapidated housing. Before major commercialization, rapping and working the turntables with a good beat became the central medium for African-American and Latino youth to voice frustration about the state of their lives in urban centers. Themes of poverty, police brutality, and the influx of drugs coupled with decreasing access to jobs, proper housing, and educational opportunities were expressed over beats, through ciphers, and and in battles. Today, hip-hop culture is a mainstream multibillion-dollar global industry, created out of the resistance movements that defined African-American history.

The excessive and discriminatory overpolicing of black people has been a central theme in America, from Jim Crow-era lynchings to the death of Eric Garner. Social media has illuminated previously unheard black voices, building mass resistance and consciousness and helping create radical national change for African Americans. The year 2014 saw the culmination of social media activism through massive nonviolent public marches and

[
Articulations of gender and class struggle were well defined in the Black Feminist movement of the 70s. African-American women and their allies of color spoke truth to power about the monopoly over gender rights in the U.S.-based Second Wave of Feminism.
]

protest. In a similar fashion to the Arab Spring in Tunisia and Egypt in 2010 and 2011, global support appeared through Twitter, Facebook, and Instagram for #BlackLivesMatter. Protesting the killings of unarmed black men—Trayvon Martin, Mike Brown, and Eric Garner, in particular—#BlackLivesMatter has emerged as a defining movement of the 21st century. African-American resistance, now more than ever, pushes against institutionalized racial inequities in the United States.

DARING TO DREAM THE LEGACY OF MLK

AMERICA'S PREEMINENT ADVOCATE FOR NONVIOLENCE

Martin Luther King Jr., born Michael Luther King Jr. on January 15, 1929, was raised in the African-American Baptist Church. He was the grandson of the Rev. A. D. Williams King, pastor of the Ebenezer Baptist Church and a founder of the NAACP's Atlanta chapter. Martin Luther King Sr. inherited the role from his own father, who was also a Civil Rights leader. King Jr. graduated from Morehouse College in Atlanta, Georgia in 1948 with a Bachelor of Arts in Sociology. After three years at Crozer Theological Seminary in Pennsylvania, he was awarded a Bachelor of Divinity in 1951. He earned his doctorate in Systematic Theology from Boston University in 1955, two years after he married Coretta Scott King. They had four children—Yolanda, Martin (III), Dexter, and Bernice. The 25-year-old King decided against the professorial route and returned to the South to become pastor of Dexter Avenue Baptist Church in Montgomery, Alabama.

King faced criticism from peers for his nonviolent philosophy in a world becoming increasingly hostile to African Americans.

Brought up as a staunch advocate for civil and human rights, King took leadership of the Montgomery Improvement Association, the central organization for the bus boycotts after Rosa Parks's arrest. While at the helm of the 1955 bus boycott, which lasted 381 days, King was subjected to arrest, house bombs, and other acts of violence, but he

BUS BOYCOTT

On December 1, 1955, in Montgomery, Alabama, Rosa Parks refused to give her seat on the bus to a white passenger. This triggered the year-long Montgomery Bus Boycott. By 1956, the Supreme Court ruled that bus segregation was unconstitutional.

never lost his resolve to nonviolently resist oppression.

By 1954, King was an executive committee member of the NAACP, and he became president of of the Southern Christian Leadership Conference (SCLC) in 1957. While the Civil Rights movement was sweeping the Southern United States, King emphasized black voting rights in his inspiring speeches. In 1958 he published his first book, *Stride Toward Freedom: The Montgomery Story*, and toured India in April 1959 to gain a deeper understanding of Mahatma Gandhi's nonviolent resistance principles. Reflecting on his trip, King stated, "Since being in India, I am more convinced than ever before that the method of nonviolent resistance is the most potent weapon available to oppressed people in their struggle for justice and human dignity." Veteran African-American activist Bayard Rustin served as King's primary mentor in the late 1950s. Rustin, an openly gay Christian pacifist and a follower of Gandhi's teachings, guided King to nonviolent resistance as a more viable option than self-defense in the struggle for civil rights. Later, King became a member of the Big Six, leaders of promenent Civil

Rights organizations, which included Roy Wilkens (NAACP), Whitney Young (National Urban League), A. Philip Randolph (Brotherhood of Sleeping Car Porters), John Lewis (SNCC), and James Farmer (Congress of Racial Equality).

He led the peaceful 1963 March on Washington for Jobs and Freedom, where more than 250,000 people of all races attended. He stood on the Mall in front of the Lincoln Memorial and immortalized his "I Have A Dream" speech that forever changed the nature of civil rights in the United States and the character of coalitions for progressive change worldwide. With these timeless words, King established himself as one of the greatest orators in U.S. history:

> I have a dream that one day this nation will rise up and live out the true meaning of its creed: "We hold these truths to be self-evident, that all men are created equal." I have a dream that one day on the red hills of Georgia, the sons of former slaves and the sons of former slave owners will be able to sit down together at the table of brotherhood. I have a dream that one day even the state of Mississippi, a state sweltering with the heat of injustice, sweltering with the heat of oppression, will be transformed into an oasis of freedom and justice. I have a dream that my four little children will one day live in a nation where they will not be judged by the color of their skin but by the content of their character. I have a dream today! I have a dream that one day, down in Alabama, with its vicious racists, with its governor having his lips dripping with the words of "interposition" and "nullification"—one day right there in Alabama little black boys and black girls will be able to join hands with little white boys and white girls as sisters and brothers. I have a dream today!

In 1964, King was named *Time* magazine's Man of the Year. Though admired by many, King faced criticism from some African-American peers for his nonviolent philosophy in a world becoming increasingly hostile to African Americans. Members of SNCC, as well as Malcolm X, had strong views about how to address discrimination in the United States. King and Malcolm X met briefly, when the two were leaving the Capitol Building after hearing politicians debate the 1964 Civil Rights Act. In the last years of their lives, both men started moving toward each other's philosophy. According to African-American history professor David Howard-Pitney:

> While Malcolm is moderating from his earlier position, King is becoming more militant . . . Despite their differences, both King and Malcolm X's political activism come from the same source. They were fundamentally spiritual men. While we remember them for their social and political activism, they were religious and spiritual men at their core.

During the last three years of his life, King became more radical. In 1968, King and the SCLC organized the Poor People's Campaign, committed to eradicating poverty for all Americans and fighting for economic justice, and demanding that the government guarantee an annual income for all citizens. King moved closer to Malcolm X's rhetoric when he started preaching black self-pride and wearing a "Black is Beautiful" button in 1967 and 1968. Soon, King took a more militant version of nonviolence in response to U.S. involvement in the Vietnam War.

SNCC STUDENTS STRIVING FOR NONVIOLENT CHANGE

I n 1960, under the leadership of John Lewis, the Student Non-violent Coordinating Committee (SNCC) was founded at Shaw University as an organization for black students to coordinate sit-ins and mass protests. The SNCC's power as an organization became most apparent through its involvement in freedom rides organized in the summer of 1961 by countless student volunteers, both black and white, from SNCC and the Congress of Racial Equality (CORE). Students took bus trips to the South to support new laws that prohibited segregation in interstate bus services and facilities.

Although these freedom riders were routinely attacked by angry mobs, the SNCC continued to immerse itself in voter registration efforts in Mississippi. In 1966, when Stokely Carmichael became chairman of SNCC, a shifting ideology encouraged Black Power and questioned the role of white supporters in the movement.

Above: African Americans sit in protest at a whites-only lunch counter in Nashville in 1960.

STRUGGLE AT HOME AND ABROAD

THE CIVIL RIGHTS MOVEMENT AND AFRICAN INDEPENDENCE

While African Americans faced whips, dogs, and water hoses in their march toward full civil and human rights in the United States, across the Atlantic Ocean, similar struggles for autonomy and nationhood were occurring on the African continent.

SOUTH AFRICA

One of the most enduring relationships of the 20th century was the Civil Rights movement's support of the anti-apartheid struggle in South Africa. Many black South Africans credited the fight for human rights and democracy in the United States as inspiration for their own movement towards civil rights; among them was anti-apartheid activist Steve Biko, who initiated South Africa's Black Consciousness Movement. Biko was killed by South African police in 1977, which sparked resistance within South Africa and incited a global cry against injustice.

ANC President Nelson Mandela is greeted on his arrival in Durban in 1993.

In 1960, South African police killed 69 innocent black South Africans in what came to be known as the Sharpeville Massacre. Following Sharpeville, African-American civil rights activists called for the immediate end of U.S. government support of the apartheid government in South Africa. Many African-American activists sent aid to black South Africans to assist in their self-defense, even though, at the time, the African American Civil Rights movement was not as inclined to violence as was the almost militant operations of the anti-apartheid movement. Still, 1962 saw the formation of the American Negro Leadership Conference on Africa (ANLCA) by 75 civil rights groups to lobby for "benevolent U.S. foreign policy towards Africans, especially South Africa."

In addition to his role as an anti-apartheid activist and, later, South Africa's first black present, Nelson Mandela was a symbolic brother to Martin Luther King Jr. though they never met. Both

MARCUS GARVEY

Jamaican-born Marcus Garvey inspired many with his 1920 message of Black Nationalism and Pan-Africanism. It was echoed in the activism of the 1960s as more and more African Americans sought to reconnect with their African ancestry and lent their political voices to African Liberation struggles on the continent.

men fought for the same ideal on two continents: nonviolence and diplomacy, to varying degrees, as methods in the struggle for civil and human rights.

Facing life imprisonment, just a year after King led the March on Washington and gave his famed "I Have a Dream" speech, Nelson Mandela spoke at his own trial, saying, "I have cherished the ideal of a democracy and free society in which all persons live together in harmony and with equal opportunities. It is an ideal which I hope to live for and to achieve. But if need be, it is an ideal for which I am prepared to die."

Denied a visa to visit South Africa in 1966, Martin Luther King Jr. gave a speech in New York denouncing the white South African Government:

> In South Africa today, all opposition to white supremacy is condemned as communism, and in its name, due process is destroyed. A medieval segregation is organized with 20th century efficiency and drive. A sophisticated form of slavery is imposed by a minority upon a majority which is kept in grinding poverty. The dignity of human personality is defiled; and world opinion is arrogantly defied.

Black South Africans were continually tested. In June of 1967, as the South African government attempted to send an all-white team to the Olympics, African Americans joined the movement to boycott their participation. Arthur Ashe, Ruby Dee, Bayard Rustin, Dick Gregory, and Floyd McKissick Jr. were among 30 signatories who supported banning the Olympics should the South African team be allowed to attend. The International Olympic Committee (IOC) succumbed to the pressure by African Americans and Africans, and withdrew the invitation for the South African team.

It wasn't until the 1980s, during the state of emergency in South Africa, that African-American leaders, including Randall Robinson, Jesse Jackson, and Harry Belafonte, led the movement to pressure American corporations to divest fully from South Africa. The anti-apartheid movement swept across campuses as a new generation of students sounded the clarion call against oppression of their black brothers and sisters in South Africa.

Martin Luther King Jr. was assassinated in 1968, before he could see his spiritual brother-in-arms' inauguration as South Africa's first black president in 1994. With King's widow, Coretta Scott King, alongside him at the podium, Mandela quoted King's famous words from his most famous speech: "Free at last, free at last, thank God almighty we are free at last."

MEXICO CITY

During the 1968 Olympics in Mexico City, African-American gold and bronze winners Tommie Smith and John Carlos (both track and field athletes), respectively, expressed global solidarity in an act of defiance that visually resonated around the world, especially with South Africans fighting for liberation. With their medals around their necks, as the "Star Spangled Banner" began to play, both men lowered their heads and raised black-gloved fists in the air in the Black Power salute, challenging the world to recognize their courage, strength, athletic prowess, *and* commitment to civil rights.

Though millions of Americans were outraged by their subversive gesture, many more people were emboldened and inspired by these men. At the risk of their careers, they stood before the world, unafraid to express their disillusionment with the United States for the mistreatment they received as African Americans. Both men were ultimately suspended from the U.S. team. Their transformative actions were a call for global awakening against all forms of racism and discrimination, shedding light on the African-American struggle in the wake of Martin Luther King Jr.'s 1968 assassination.

SIR SIDNEY POITIER

I n 1964, Sir Sidney Poitier was the first black Academy Award winner for Best Actor for his role in *Lilies of the Field*, a breakthrough that revolutionized the acting world for black Americans. Born in Florida to Bahamian parents in 1927, Poitier moved to New York to pursue an acting career. He joined the American Negro Theater and made his acting debut in a production of *Days of Our Youth*. After years of working on stage, Poitier made his Hollywood start in 1950 in *No Way Out*. His leading roles in *Porgy and Bess* and *A Raisin in the Sun* turned him into a star and an inspiration. Breaking the color barrier in film, Poitier used his fame to support the Civil Rights movement of the 1960s. In 1974 he was appointed a Knight Commander of the British Empire, granting him the title Sir. After a series of big-screen films, Poitier retired from acting and published his memoir, *The Measure of a Man*, in 2000. Among countless awards for his international diplomacy, in 2009 Poitier was awarded the Presidential Medal of Freedom by President Obama.

CELEBRITIES GIVE VOICE TO THE STRUGGLE

WHAT GOOD IS FAME WITHOUT RIGHTS?

From Sammy Davis Jr. and Jackie Robinson to Harry Belafonte and Muhammad Ali, countless African Americans pioneered the integration of the public stages of entertainment and sports, using their voices to support the Civil Rights movement. Risking fame and fortune, a number of black celebrities used their popularity to fight injustice and highlight the black experience in America.

JACKIE ROBINSON

Jackie Robinson made his baseball debut at Ebbets Field in Brooklyn, New York, in front of almost 27,000 fans. Throughout his career, he was subjected to racial taunts on and off the field. Even so, he helped the Dodgers win the National League pennant in 1947, securing the title of Rookie of the Year. By 1949, he was voted the National League's most valuable player. In many interviews, Robinson spoke about breaking the color barrier as the first African American in Major League Baseball, which had been segregated for more than 50 years. After a distinguished 10-year baseball career, he retired from the game and focused on civil rights activism, working with the NAACP, King's SCLC, and the Student Emergency Fund to advance the Civil Rights movement. As the Chairman of the Freedom Fund, which raised millions of dollars in support of the movement, Robinson stated, "Certainly if such revolutionary change can be brought about in baseball, it can also be brought about in education, in transportation, and

DID YOU KNOW

In 1946, Jackie Robinson (1919–1972) was the first African-American baseball player to integrate baseball when he signed with the Brooklyn Dodgers baseball team. He played with their farm team in Montreal. Six days before the start of the 1947 season, Robinson was called up to the major leagues to play first baseman.

any other area of our American life." He participated in countless marches, including the 1963 March on Washington for Jobs and Freedom.

SAMMY DAVIS JR.

Sammy Davis Jr. was born in Harlem, New York, on December 8, 1925. Though small in stature, his talents made him larger than life. As a singer, dancer, author, comedian, and musician, he grew up with a father and grandfather who were already part of the 1930s entertainment world. Shielded by his parents from the world of racism, Davis eventually encountered it when he joined the U.S. Army in 1942. He became part of an integrated entertainment unit and used his talent to protect himself from the military's rampant hate and prejudice. He was discharged after serving two years.

In 1954 Davis was involved in a car accident, which nearly cost him his life. He lost the use of his left eye and as a result, he wore a glass eye until his death. However, his popularity increased. His controversial conversion to Judaism sparked discussion among black and white Americans. As a black man, Davis consistently challenged racialized social codes and widespread discrimination. As his solo career flourished, he became involved in an interracial relationship that almost cost him

[
$100,000: the amount Belafonte was tasked to deliver to Greenwood SNCC during Belafonte's first visit to Mississippi during the Freedom Summer of 1964.
]

everything. Mixed-race relationships were taboo on and off the screen in Hollywood; they were illegal in 31 states.

In 1959, Davis became part of the famous Rat Pack, with Frank Sinatra, Dean Martin, Joey Bishop, Peter Lawford, Shirley MacLaine, and Angie Dickinson. Davis made three movies with the group, but he felt the sting of Jim Crow even at the height of his performances. While he could work the stages of hotels and casinos, he could not stay in the hotels, gamble, eat at the restaurants, or drink at the bars, which were all segregated. Davis was in similar company with other trail-blazing African Americans of the time, including Dorothy Dandridge, Nat King Cole, Count Basie, and Johnny Mathis. When Davis married Swedish actress May Britt on November 13, 1960, it caused a split throughout the United States. Blacks felt that he sold out the Civil Rights movement while whites felt he had overstepped his boundaries, which cost him numerous fans.

Davis's commitment and activism in the Civil Rights movement defied expectations. With his soaring career, he used his muscle to demand that the new generation of African-American performers would not face the same discrimination that he had. He refused to play venues that were not integrated; if they wanted him, they had to allow African-American performers full access to the same accommodations and services as their white peers. Davis lent his voice and vision, supporting the struggle for full dignity for African Americans in entertainment. He died in 1990 from throat cancer, receiving many honors and awards during his life and after. Davis was inducted posthumously into the International Civil Rights Walk of Fame.

MUHAMMAD ALI

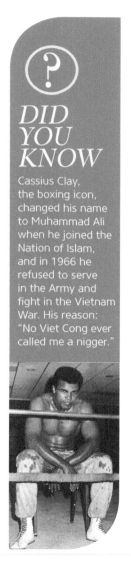

DID YOU KNOW

Cassius Clay, the boxing icon, changed his name to Muhammad Ali when he joined the Nation of Islam, and in 1966 he refused to serve in the Army and fight in the Vietnam War. His reason: "No Viet Cong ever called me a nigger."

Muhammad Ali, (Cassius Marcellus Clay Jr.), was born on January 17, 1942, in Louisville, Kentucky. He is the most iconic heavyweight boxer of all time. At the age of 12, Ali began training at Columbia Gym with boxing coach Joe Martin. Ali took training very seriously, balancing school while training six days a week. Competing in the 1960 Olympics, he defeated Polish champion Zbigniew Pietrzykowski and was awarded the gold medal. Known for his theatrical flair and quickness, Ali would taunt his opponents with his legendary line, "Float like a butterfly, sting like a bee." His 1964 fight against Sonny Liston crowned Ali as the heavyweight boxing champion of the world.

The day after the Liston fight, Ali announced his conversion to the Nation of Islam (NOI) and the change of his name from Clay to Ali. In the 1960s, Ali won every match and became a cultural symbol of black pride and power. Ali maintained a close relationship with Malcolm X as a member of NOI, using his celebrity to speak out about the civil rights struggle. Leaving NOI to convert to

Sunni Islam in 1975, Ali symbolized the great personal sacrifice, going to great lengths to maintain his principles against violence. In 1967, Ali was drafted for the Vietnam War. He refused to go, protesting on religious grounds in his belief against killing. Ali reminded the world that the Vietnamese weren't the ones who attacked him with dogs and water hoses, dehumanizing acts perpetrated by a U.S. government that degraded black Americans as second-class citizens. These sentiments did not help his cause, and he was found guilty of draft evasion and was fined, arrested, and banned from boxing, as well as stripped of his title for more than three and a half years. After the Supreme Court exonerated him in 1971, Ali returned to the ring and won the heavyweight championship three times, becoming the first person in history to do so.

HARRY BELAFONTE

Harry Belafonte (Harold George Bellanfanti Jr.) was born on March 1, 1927, in New York to Jamaican parents. Musician, actor, and human rights activist, Belafonte joined the Civil Rights movement in the 1950s, becoming a close confidant to Martin Luther King Jr. Over the years, Belafonte organized and funded major demonstrations. His 1956 breakthrough album, *Calypso,* which featured his signature "Banana Boat Song," became the first full-length album to sell more than one million copies. He became the first African American to win an Emmy, in 1959, for his TV special, *Revlon Revue: Tonight with Belafonte.* He was known to say, "Civil rights is not a movement, it is a way of life."

Belafonte financed Freedom Rides, supported voter registration, raised thousands of dollars to release King and others from jail, and helped organize the 1963 March on Washington. After King's death, Belafonte continued to fight for human rights, riding the global impact of the Civil Rights movement. In his current activism, he strives for dignity of all people who continue to fight for freedom. In reflecting on the Civil Rights movement, Belafonte stated:

> We were looking to integrate into America, whether it was racial integration or some type of social integration. It was that we knew that if we were not part of the fabric of what this nation professed to be about, that if we didn't have the right to vote, that if we didn't have the right to attend institutions of our choice for learning, that if we didn't have the chance to become a bigger part of the American dream that was, for us, also a dream, that we would never really truly touch the heartbeat of what America was about. This was about a bigger integration . . . .What black people have always wanted was not that we were rushing to become racially integrated. That was not really what the mission was about. But the specific target was to shape the economic paradigm.

In speaking about King, Belafonte mused, "One of the things that consistently nourished my commitment to Dr. King was his honesty. The fact that he remained eternally vulnerable because he always was in question about his right to lead, his right to make decisions and do things that could have such an impact on human life."

WA-ALAIKUM-SALAAM

MALCOLM X AND
THE NATION OF ISLAM

Malcolm X was born as Malcolm Little on May 19, 1925, in Omaha, Nebraska. His father, Earl Little, was a supporter of Marcus Garvey and raised his children with a deep commitment to civil rights activism. In 1931, Little was murdered by the white supremist group the Black Legion in Lansing, Michigan, where he had moved his family

Above: Malcolm X holds up a paper for the crowd to see during a black Muslim rally in New York City on August 6, 1963.

in 1929. Malcolm's mother, Louise Little, suffered an emotional breakdown and was hospitalized, leaving her children to fend for themselves in foster homes and orphanages. Malcolm eventually moved to Boston, where he lived with his half-sister, Ella, and began a life of hustling on the streets of Roxbury.

Later, lured by the thrill of the Harlem Renaissance in New York, Malcolm engaged in drug dealing, pimping, gambling, and breaking into expensive houses. Called "Detroit Red" because of his conked red hair, Malcolm was arrested and convicted on burglary charges in 1946. He was sentenced to 10 years in prison, though he was granted parole after seven years.

With his brilliance and charisma, Malcolm moved quickly up the ranks of the NOI.

During his time in prison, Malcolm began a journey of self-education. Inspired by his brother Reginald's recent conversion to the Nation of Islam (NOI), Malcolm began studying the teachings of NOI leader Elijah Muhammad. Malcolm started reading and copying the dictionary to learn to write legible letters to Muhammad from prison, expressing interest in the NOI. After studying the dictionary, he read books in the prison library, which spanned global history, philosophy, and literature. A new world opened for Malcolm. He revealed that during his seven years in prison, he became a disciplined scholar who used this time for

> **In 1995,** a million black men gathered in Washington, DC, under the leadership of NOI's Minister Louis Farrakhan for the first Million Man March and Day of Atonement. Black men from all creeds and classes came together to publicly atone for their failures and accept responsibility as the family members.

self-improvement; essentially, he gained a college education from his prison cell. Reflecting on his education, Malcolm stated, "My alma mater was books, a good library . . . . I could spend the rest of my life reading, just satisfying my curiosity."

ENTERING ISLAM

Elijah Muhammad argued that African Americans would only prosper if they lived separately from white Americans. He supported African American-owned schools, businesses, markets, NOI mosques, NOI marriages, and a clear code of conduct for all NOI members. By the time he was paroled, in 1952, Malcolm was a devoted follower of Elijah Muhammad and the NOI. He changed his name to X to replace his "slave name," Little.

With his brilliance and charisma, Malcolm moved quickly up the ranks of the NOI and was appointed a minister and NOI national spokesman. He became responsible for opening new mosques in Detroit and Harlem. Malcolm was credited with having increased membership in the NOI from 500 in 1952 to 30,000 by 1963. African Americans from all over the United States were captivated by his message of self-respect, dignity, and self-actualization.

Always thoughtful and full of humor, Malcolm X took the media by storm. His position on NOI philosophy, taken directly

ONE LIFE STORY

In 1963, Malcolm began collaboration with Alex Haley (author of Roots*) on his life story,* The Autobiography of Malcolm X. *He told Haley, "If I'm alive when this book comes out, it will be a miracle." Malcolm X was shot to death by Nation of Islam members on February 21, 1965. The autobiography was published later that year.*

from Elijah Muhammad's teachings, was discussed during a week-long television special with journalist Mike Wallace in 1959 called "The Hate that Hate Produced." During this show, Malcolm's famous declarations about the "white man being the devil" hit the front of newspapers countrywide. As his star began to eclipse Elijah Muhammad's leadership, Malcolm's celebrity became feared by white America. The NOI was infiltrated by the FBI.

Malcolm remained a faithful and devout member of the NOI, with Elijah Muhammad as his surrogate father until, at the height of the Civil Rights movement in 1963, he was betrayed by Muhammad. Muhammad had been having illicit relationships with at least six women within the organization and had fathered several children. While preaching celibacy, faithfulness, and self-control, Muhammad had blatantly abused his own powers and acted against the principles he put in place. Malcolm refused to keep Muhammad's indiscretions secret, as he

....

✳ **The Autobiography of Malcolm X**
is one of *Time* magazine's Ten Most Important Nonfiction Books of the 20th Century.

....

was devastated by Muhammad's weakness. Malcolm's faith was shaken as he also took responsibility for attracting hundreds to join the NOI, which he felt was a fraudulent organization.

Muhammad saw a way to silence Malcolm for 90 days after a public comment Malcolm X made concerning President Kennedy's assassination on November 22, 1963, stating, "Kennedy never foresaw that the chickens would come home to roost." The comment was taken out of context, yet it was Muhammad's perfect opportunity to bring Malcolm down a notch. Understanding that he was being punished for larger issues beyond the Kennedy comment, Malcolm left the NOI in March 1964 and formed his own organization, the Muslim Mosque Inc.

Malcolm changed his name to El Hajj Malik El-Shabazz to indicate he had completed the Hajj, the ritual pilgrimage to Mecca. From Africa, he wrote a letter to a friend, saying:

My journey is almost ended, and I have a much broader scope than when I started out, which I believe will add new life and dimensions to our struggle for freedom and honor and dignity in the States. I am writing these things so that you will now for a fact the tremendous sympathy and support we have among the African states for our human rights struggle. The main thing is that we keep a united front wherein our most valuable time and energy will not be wasted fighting each other.

This was a major shift from his philosophy under the NOI and Elijah Muhammad. Treated as a dignitary in his travels throughout Africa and the Middle East, Malcolm encountered people of all races who prayed with him and supported his struggle for African Americans in the United States. His growing Pan-Africanist philosophy was the impetus for the creation of the secular Organization of Afro-American Unity (OAAU).

ESCAPING ELIJAH MUHAMMAD'S SHADOW

Author and theologian James Cone explained, "King was a political revolutionary. Malcolm was a cultural revolutionary. Malcolm changed how black people thought about themselves. Before Malcolm came along, we were all Negroes. After Malcolm, he helped us become black." In July 1964, Malcolm X spoke at the OAAU, starting, "In the interest of world peace, we beseech the heads of the independent African states to recommend an immediate investigating into our problem by the United Nations Commission on Human Rights."

Malcolm felt that the African-American freedom struggle needed to be taken out of the hands of the U.S. government because it was not only a civil rights issue but a violation of human rights. It was at the United Nations, facing global leaders, where Malcolm felt that charges against the United States for human-rights violations of African Americans were best pursued. Malcolm reasoned that if countries around the world could condemn the mistreatment of black South Africans under apartheid, then surely they would not remain silent about the brutality against African Americans. Malcolm wanted to work with any willing leaders to file the charge.

Although he was an esteemed global leader for African-American rights, Malcolm did not feel safe in the United States. After repeated attempts on his life, Malcolm was forced to travel with bodyguards. In February 1965, his house in East Elmhurst, New York, where he lived with his wife, Betty, and their four daughters, was firebombed. They managed to escape unharmed.

A week later, while speaking at the Audubon Ballroom in Manhattan on February 21, 1965, Malcolm was shot 21 times at close range. Malcolm X, age 39, was pronounced dead on arrival at New York's Columbia Presbyterian Hospital. Three members of the NOI were convicted of first-degree murder in March 1966. More than 1,500 people attended Malcolm's funeral in Harlem, New York, on February 27, 1965, at the Faith Temple Church of God in Christ. Actor Ossie Davis delivered an impassioned eulogy, forever preserving the legacy of Malcolm's life:

> Here—at this final hour, this quiet place—Harlem has come to bid farewell to one of is brightest hopes—extinguished now, and gone from us forever. . . . Malcolm was our manhood, our living black manhood. This was his meaning to his people. And, in honoring him, we honor the best in ourselves. . . . Consigning these mortal remains to earth, the common mother of all, secure in the knowledge that what we place in the ground is no more than a man— but a seed—which, after the winter of our discontent, will come forth again to meet us. And we will know him then for what he was and is—a Prince—our own black shining Prince!—who didn't hesitate to do, because he loved us so.

DISAPPOINTMENT AND DESIRE

A RISE IN BLACK POWER AFTER MLK AND MALCOLM X

After the assassinations of Malcolm X on February 21, 1965, and Martin Luther King Jr. on April 4, 1968, a shift in philosophy occurred among African Americans. Heeding Stokely Carmichael's call for Black Power, alliances and coalitions were created that moved away from King's nonviolent resistance platform. New organizations focused on the improvement of black communities while advocating self-defense in the face of police brutality. The most salient group of the late 1960s that advocated a Black Power philosophy was the Black Panther Party for Self-Defense (BPP). The BPP was an African-American revolutionary party founded on October 15, 1966, by Huey P. Newton and Bobby Seale in Oakland, California. Its initial purpose was to serve as a community watchdog group that would patrol African-American neighborhoods and protect black people from police brutality. It evolved into a Marxist-based party calling for the need for African Americans to arm themselves in self-defense, government reparations for slavery, the release of all African Americans from the prison system, and exemption from the military draft, among other measures. The BPP made clear that it was an autonomous group with no association to Marcus

BPP was an African-American revolutionary party.

Left: American revolutionary and educator Angela Davis shortly after she was fired from her post as philosophy professor at UCLA in 1969 due to her membership in the Communist Party of America.

Garvey's Universal Negro Improvement Association (UNIA) or the Nation of Islam (NOI). Unlike other African-American cultural nationalists groups, which favored total segregation, the BPP willingly worked alongside non racist whites and other progressive allies in the United States. Focused on the eradication of poverty and the liberty of working-class people, the BPP would not tolerate African-American elites who exploited others, including their African-American brothers and sisters. The BPP outlined its Ten Point Program (right), focused on alleviating unjust economic conditions.

The BPP believed that only the abolition of capitalism would end economic exploitation as the cause of oppression in the United States and abroad and achieve social justice. As its socialist outlook resonated with movements around the world, FBI director J. Edgar Hoover pronounced the BPP the greatest threat to national security in 1969. The BPP became a central interest of the FBI's counterintelligence program, COINTELPRO. The BPP gained instant fame and new members throughout the nation after its televised 1967 march (dressed in their uniforms of guns, black berets, and black leather jackets) into the California State Legislature in Sacramento to protest a gun-control bill called the Mulford Act , which repealed a law allowing citizens to publicly carry loaded firearms.

Committed to serving the black community, the BPP launched more than 35 Survival Programs and provided the community with education, legal aid, transportation assistance, and the manufacture and distribution of free shoes for poor people. Its most successful program was the Free Breakfast Program, which fed thousands of school children daily. However, Hoover used all his resources in COINTELPRO to unravel the organization,

Black Power Party
Ten-Point Program

1 We want Freedom. We want power to determine the destiny of our Black Community.

2 We want full employment of our people.

3 We want an end to the robbery by the white man of our Community.

4 We want decent housing, fit for the shelter of human beings.

5 We want education for our people that exposes the true nature of this decadent American society. We want education that teaches us our true history and our role in the present-day society.

6 We want all black men to be exempt from military service.

7 We want an immediate end to police brutality and murder of black people.

8 We want freedom for all black men held in federal, state, county, and city prisons and jails.

9 We want all black people when brought to trial to be tried in court by a jury of their peer group or people from their black communities, as defined by the Constitution of the United States.

10 We want land, bread, housing, education, clothing, justice, and peace. And as our major political objective, a United Nations-supervised plebiscite to be held throughout the black colony in which only black colonial subjects will be allowed to participate, for the purpose of determining the will of black people as to their national destiny. **POWER TO THE PEOPLE.**

as he claimed its members were communists and homeland terrorists. The FBI led a concerted effort to infiltrate, imprison, spread misinformation, sabotage, and use deadly force against BPP leaders which included such influential leaders as Huey P. Newton, Bobby Seale, Stokely Carmichael, Fred Hampton, Angela Davis, and Assata Shakur.

HUEY P. NEWTON, cofounder of the BPP, was born on February 17, 1942, in Monroe, Louisiana, but grew up in Oakland, California. A voracious reader, Newton understood that the education he received in public school was not adequate. He began a path of self-education, reading the works of Plato, Mao Zedong, Che Guevara, Karl Marx, Malcolm X, and Vladimir Lenin to form his own political ideology.

As a student at Merritt College, he started the Black Panther Party for Self Defense in 1966. While Bobby Seale was elected chairman of the party, Newton became minister of defense. Newton published his autobiography, *Revolutionary Suicide*, in 1973. Newton's driving philosophy was called "revolutionary humanism." He earned his PhD in history from the University of California-Santa Cruz in 1980. After the unraveling of the BPP through FBI pressure and internal strife (and a charge against Newton for embezzlement of $600,000 in state funds), Newton disbanded the BPP in 1982.

Tragically, in 1989, he was murdered on a street corner in Oakland by a drug dealer in the same neighborhood where he and Seale began many of their survival programs that sought to better the black community.

BOBBY SEALE, (Robert George Seale) was born on October 22, 1936, in Dallas. As co-founder of the BPP with Huey Newton,

Bill Whitfield, member of the Black Panther chapter in Kansas City, serves free breakfast to children before they go to school, April 16, 1969.

Seale maintained a doctrine of militant black empowerment. His political aspirations were formed when he heard Malcolm X speak at a public meeting in 1962 at Merritt College in Oakland. In 1968, Seale was charged with conspiring to incite riots around the Democratic National Convention and was sentenced to four years in prison for 16 counts of contempt of court. After his release from prison in 1972, Seale distanced himself from the BPP and concentrated on working within the system for community change. Reflecting on his time in the BPP, Seale shared, "From 1962 to 1965, the Black Panther Party was based on a complete study and research of African and African-American people's history of struggle . . . . In terms of the concept of economics at the time, what I developed best was a concept of community controlled cooperatives in the black community, which largely I picked up from W. E. B. Dubois."

Angela Davis (far right) attends her first news conference on February 24, 1972, after being released on bail.

ANGELA DAVIS, was born on January 26, 1944, in Birmingham, Alabama. As a young student, she traveled to Europe on several occasions, where she met revolutionary youth from around the world. Fascinated by the philosophy of Karl Marx and communism, she differed greatly from Stokely Carmichael, who felt that Marxism was a white man's tool. Davis believed socialism was the tool to liberate blacks. In 1968, she joined the Black Panther Party of Los Angeles. She maintained close ties to Carmichael's SNCC and helped create the SNCC Youth Corps. Devastated in 1968 by King's assassination, Davis joined the Che-Lumumba Club, the black cell of the Communist Party, an important turning point that made public her association with communism. That year, she began a doctoral program at University of California–San Diego.

In 1970, she became involved with Soledad Brother George Jackson's prison case, in which she was accused of providing weapons for an attempted escape, an accusation that placed Davis on the FBI's Most Wanted List. She was imprisoned in New York for several months; while incarcerated, she got an intimate, eye-opening view of the horrific conditions inside the prison system. She articulated her views on communism and was moved to California, where her case was tried. After two years of incarceration, Davis was released on a not-guilty ruling in June 1972. Out of prison, Davis returned to life as an academic, teaching at San Francisco State University and Claremont College. Though not successful, she ran for vice president of the Communist Party in 1980 and 1984. Davis became an international voice against gender discrimination, exemplified in her feelings about the exclusion

✳ **Stokely Carmichael,** who later changed his name to Kwame Ture, was a Trinidadian American Pan-Africanist.

of women during the 1995 Million Man March on Washington, DC. The author of several books, Davis has become a world icon for her activism. She is a cofounder of Critical Resistance, a national grass-roots organization fighting the injustices of the prison-industrial system. Together with scholar Kimberle Crenshaw, she formed the African-American Agenda 2000, an alliance of black feminists.

In solidarity with those against the death penalty, Davis has lent her support to fight sexism, racism, and the corruption of the criminal justice system. She continues to lecture around the world on these issues.

FRED HAMPTON, born on August 30, 1948, in Summit, Illinois, was chairman of the Illinois chapter of the Black Panther Party and the deputy chair of the National Black Panther Party. As a student, Hampton became active in the Civil Rights movement and joined the NAACP. He was appointed leader of the NAACP Youth Council of the organization's West Suburban branch, and he formed the Chicago chapter of the Black Panther Party in November 1968. Along with community service programs that offered free medical clinics and breakfast for school children, Hampton rallied for a truce between Chicago's most powerful street gangs. In May 1969, he held a press conference citing a non aggression pact among the gangs and the creation of a "rainbow coalition" of youth from all races. Hoover's FBI turned its attention to all BPP chapters and focused on Hampton's branch.

In 1969 the Chicago office was raided three times, with more than 100 members arrested. On December 4, 1969, during a fourth raid of the BPP Chicago headquarters, police killed Fred Hampton, who was 21 years old.

ASSATA SHAKUR, born Joanne Deborah Chesimard, is the godmother of the Black Liberation Army (BLA) and was a member of the Black Panther Party. She was arrested while resisting police in a shoot-out on the New Jersey Turnpike in May 1973. Shakur's companion in the car, Zayd Shakur, was killed, along with a state trooper. The third person in the car, Sundiata Acoli, is still serving a life sentence in prison. Assata was convicted by an all-white jury in 1977 and sentenced to life in prison. After giving birth to her daughter in prison, Shakur escaped on November 2, 1979. She was granted political asylum in Cuba in 1986 and has resided there ever since.

CONSCIOUS ON CAMPUS

KARENGA AND 1960S COLLEGIATE ACTIVISM

Maulana Karenga, activist, professor, and chair of Africana Studies at California State University–Long Beach, holds two PhDs and is the founder of the Kawaida Institute of Pan-African Studies in Los Angeles. He is also the national chairman of the Organization Us, a cultural and social change organization. Karenga played a seminal role in shaping and supporting the 1960s Black Arts and Black Power movements while helping establish black studies programs in U.S. colleges and universities. Karenga has always maintained that African Americans must have a connection to their culture to create solidarity and overcome oppression.

Karenga is best known as the creator of Kwanzaa, a week-long African-American celebration between Christmas and New Year that focuses on the Nguzo Saba (Seven Principles), which affirm African-American commitments to self, family, and community. Kwanzaa was created from the African philosophical framework of Kawaida, which Karenga defines as "an ongoing synthesis of the best of African thought and practice in constant exchange with the world." Kwanzaa's seven principles include: Umoja (Unity), Kujichagulia (Self-Determination), Ujima (Collective Work and Responsibility), Ujamaa (Cooperative Economics), Nia (Purpose), Kuumba (Creativity), and Imani (Faith).

Karenga's influence was felt throughout the 1960s on college campuses. Student activism was at a high as protests mounted against American involvement in the Vietnam War. One of the most memorable campus gatherings was on October 29, 1966, at the University of California–Berkeley's Greek Theater, where more than 10,000 people gathered to hear Stokely Carmichael give his now-famous "Black Power" speech, which defined Black Power as a "psychological battle for the right of black people to define their own terms, define themselves as they see fit, and organize as they see it."

Carmichael gave clear advice to white students on how they could overcome their own racism to create a more equitable United States. His message of Black Power and Pan-Africanism became a clarion call across campuses.

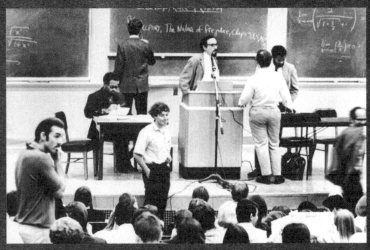

Black Panther leader Eldridge Cleaver (seated, at desk) prepares to give his first lecture in Social Analysis 139X, an experimental course on race and racism at UC Berkeley (1968).

MATCHING A MOVEMENT

BLACK ARTS MEET BLACK POWER

The Black Arts Movement (BAM) originated from the Black Power concept that African-American writer Richard Wright coined to define African independence struggles in the late 1950s. Stokely Carmichael, chairman of the SNCC, used the term again in the 1960s, and it quickly became the buzzword for emerging black liberation struggles in the United States. Black theater groups, poetry performances, and journal publications were hallmarks of Black Arts activity. The movement took place from roughly 1965 to 1976. BAM was the only literary movement in the United States whose social engagement was based within black and brown communities throughout the nation, and its civil rights protest literature produced an alternative theme: Black Power.

In a 1968 essay, African-American theater scholar Larry Neal wrote that the Black Arts Movement was the "aesthetic and spiritual sister of the Black Power concept." Poet Amiri Baraka (LeRoi Jones) was the founder of the movement, establishing it after the assassination of Malcolm X in 1965. Along with James Baldwin and Ishmael Reed, Baraka was one of the most widely published black writers of BAM. Some of BAM's founding members include

American poet Yolanda Cornelia "Nikki" Giovanni at her desk in 1973.

Larry Neal, Amiri Baraka, Sonia Sanchez, Nikki Giovanni, and Askia Ture, among others. They were the vanguard of artistic activism that swept across the United States as the fever of Black Power was catching fire.

The BAM encouraged black artists to write about their own history, traditions, and cultures. *Umbra* magazine became the first black literary publication with a distinguished and distinct voice separate from the white literary canon.

In 1967, Baraka visited Karenga in Los Angeles and became an advocate for his principal of Kawaida. Askia Ture, a visiting

BLACK FIRE

Published in 1968, Black Fire, edited by Amiri Baraka and Larry Neal, stands as the definitive anthology documenting the first wave of poets (Amiri Baraka, Nikki Giovanni, Haki Madhubuti, Sonia Sanchez—above), playwrights (Ed Mullins and Ron Milner), and literary critic (Hoyt Fuller) in the Black Arts Movement.

professor at San Francisco State University, would become the most influential poet-professor of BAM. Playwright Ed Bullins established the Black Arts West, and editor Dingane Goncalves founded the *Journal of Black Poetry* in 1966. The nucleus of Bullins, Goncalves, Baraka, Sonia Sanchez, Askia Ture, and Marvin X became the center of the Black Arts leadership.

Black theaters became sites for artistic production while doubling as venues for community meetings, lectures, study groups, and film screenings. A distinct national identity was created as cultural centers all over the United States began focusing on Black Arts' roots in activism with Black Power as its philosophy. Some of the Black Arts theaters across the nation included the New Lafayette Theater and the National Black Theatre in New York; Baraka's Spirit House Movers in Newark; Kuumba Theater Company in Chicago; Black Arts Midwest in Detroit; and in Los Angeles, the Ebony Showcase, Inner City Repertory Company, and the Performing Arts City of LA.

✳ **Black Arts Repertory Theatre School**
(BARTS) was founded in 1965 by Amiri Baraka (LeRoi Jones).

The widespread publication and distribution of Black Arts magazines helped promote and sustain the movement. For the first time, writers were being read, critiqued, and published by black publishers for a primarily black audience. Unlike the literary production of the Harlem Renaissance, there were virtually no wealthy white patrons funding black writers. The first major Black Arts publication was *Black Dialogue*, published in 1964 in California. Dingane Goncalves became the poetry editor for *Black Dialogue* and also started the *Journal of Black Poetry*. The first journal of black studies and research, *Black Scholar*, was published in 1969. For creative writing, the most important publication was the *Negro Digest/Black World*, put out by the Johnson family, the publishers of *Ebony* and *Jet* magazines.

BAM dissolved in 1974 due to government pressure and internal strife. As independent publishers and political activists based in the community, BAM leaders could not compete with corporate funding, which handpicked certain black writers and playwrights into the mainstream, primarily for Broadway.

LEAVING A LEGACY

LARRY NEAL was one of the most influential scholars and writers of the BAM. Born in 1937 in Atlanta, he is considered the leading theoretician of the Black Aesthetic. Neal reflected on the political influence of Malcolm X on the formation of BAM, stating, "My ears were more attuned to the music of urban black America—the blues idiom music called jazz. Malcolm was like that music. He reminded many of us of the music of Charlie Parker and John Coltrane—a music that was a central force in the emerging ethos of the black artistic consciousness."

Neal, more than any other writer at the time, articulated the connections between the Black Arts Movement, Black Power, and black history.

AMIRI BARAKA (LeRoi Jones) had a writing career that spanned 50 years, most of which challenged white racism and supported black liberation. As a founder of BARTS and a pioneer of the Black Arts Movement, Baraka explored the anger of African Americans facing their disenfranchisement in the United States by using his poetry as a weapon against racism. A world-respected poet and playwright, Baraka was one of the revolutionary activists who dedicated his life to fighting for the rights of African Americans.

NIKKI GIOVANNI (Yolanda Cornelia Nikki Giovanni) was born in 1943 in Knoxville, Tennessee. She began writing poetry in the 1960s as a member of the Black Arts Movement. Now a world-renowned poet, activist, and educator, Giovanni was dubbed the "princess of Black Poetry" by the *New York Times* early in her career. The author of more than 30 books for adults and children, Giovanni has committed her work to the fight for civil rights and equality.

SONIA SANCHEZ (Wilsonia Benita Driver) was born on September 9, 1934, in Birmingham, Alabama. She earned a Bachelor of Arts in Political Science from Hunter College of the City University of New York in 1955. As a member of Congress of Racial Equality (CORE), her philosophy on integration radically changed after hearing Malcolm X speak. His influence on black self-definition helped shape her work. Along with Nikki Giovanni and Etheridge Knight, Sanchez formed the Broadside Quartet of young poets while running a writers' workshop in Greenwich Village. She was instrumental in establishing the first black studies program in the country, along with Nathan Hare, at San Francisco State University. Between 1972 and 1975, Sanchez joined the Nation of Islam, but left because of gender inequities. Author of more than a dozen books of poetry and published plays, Sanchez was the first Presidential Fellow at Temple University, where she taught from 1977 until her retirement in 1999.

ASKIA MUHAMMAD TURE, though not widely known outside of BAM circles, was a member of the New York–based Umbra literary group and a writer for *Liberator Magazine*. Amiri Baraka considered him the catalyst for the Black Arts Movement and served as his inspiration, along with Larry Neal, for opening the Black Arts Repertory Theatre/School. Both Neal and Ture served as mentors to Baraka in the late 1960s.

THE BLACK ARTS REPERTORY THEATRE

BARAKA MAKES A HOME FOR BAM'S BLACK AESTHETIC

Founded in 1965 by Amiri Baraka (pictured, left), The Black Arts Repertory Theatre/School (BARTS) was opened in Harlem, New York. Baraka's intention was to take black music, poetry, art, and performance out of the white academy and into the black community. The theater staged Baraka's award-winning piece *Dutchman*, which depicted the white exploitation of blacks. He inspired playwrights such as Ed Bullins to envision and create a strong black aesthetic for the stage. BARTS was the space that launched the Black Arts Movement.

AND STILL I RISE
BLACK WOMEN
IN MOVEMENT

THE POWER OF THE BLACK
FEMINIST MOVEMENT

The Black Feminist Movement was a direct response to the Black Liberation and Women's movements of the 1960s and 1970s. In speaking to the racial oppression in the Women's Movement and the sexual oppression and misogyny of the Black Liberation Struggle, black women felt that they were caught in the middle and needed a space to clearly articulate their own identities. Its origins date to the 1973 founding of the National Black Feminist Organization (NBFO) in New York and Black Women Organized for Action (BWOA).

Black women experienced deep frustration with the growing Feminist Movement, which largely comprised middle-class white women.

Within the Civil Rights and Black Power movements, SNCC, and the Black Panther Party, the freedom and liberation focused on the black male. The rhetoric in much of these movements was highly sexualized and excluded black women from powerful leadership positions. What was applied to black women in terms of conduct codes, especially concerning interracial relationships, was not applied to men, as they had "indiscriminate access to and control over any woman's body."

Within these movements, black male lives were privileged over black women's lives. Black women were constantly kept in place, reminded that they were a support, but never at the

In May 1973, The National Black Feminist Organization was founded to address both sexism and racism faced by black women. Margaret Sloan, the NBFO's president, and co-founder Michele Wallace articulated that the NFBO aimed to "raise the visibility of black women in both the Feminist and Black Liberation movements."

vanguard of change. According to *Thistle Magazine*, Amiri Baraka made public that he did not believe black men and women were equal. He stated:

> Not only are men and women different but there is no reciprocity in their relationship to each other; hence a black man is not "for" his woman as a black woman is "for" her man. The two do not submit to one another; rather, the woman submits to her black man.

Baraka also believed that it was only white people who propagated the notion of equality, since equality was against human nature.

Elaine Brown of the Black Panther Party reflected on the strict gender roles of the BPP when on one occasion the women were told to wait until all the men ate before they could get access to food that the women had contributed to making. The BPP gender code stated that "sisters did not challenge brothers. Sisters stood behind their black men, supported their men, and respected them." There were also many black women who endorsed and enforced these gender roles on black women themselves, perpetuating the silencing patriarchal modes that their male peers practiced.

Black women experienced deep frustration with the growing Feminist Movement, which comprised largely middle-class white women in the 1960s. Excluded from conferences, meetings, and leadership roles, black women rejected the attempt by white women to universalize women's experiences without including women of color in articulating their experiences with race, class, and sex. Black feminists began to create their own liberation struggle as they witnessed the white feminists' unwillingness to face issues of racism and privilege. Some white feminists, such as Adrienne Rich, claimed that white women had always been part of an anti-racist trajectory, though there is little historical proof of white women on the front lines of Black Liberation struggles. One thinks of the murder of Emmett Till, and the foundation for such an argument is dissolved.

When looking at the history of white feminist movements in the United States, most of these struggles were for the sole benefit of white women, using the black woman as the moral compass in which to uplift their own place in mainstream society.

The idea of a Black Feminist Movement in the early 1970s was easier to accept conceptually than it was to put into practice. Many black women did not want to call themselves feminist, as it was associated with the mainstream movement, which focused on women working outside the home and garnering equal pay. Black women had always worked outside the

DID YOU KNOW

The Combahee River Collective was named after the Combahee River Raid of June 1863 (led by Harriet Tubman, pictured below), which freed hundreds of slaves. The Collective had a self-defined socialist agenda that explored the shortcomings of mainstream feminism.

home while supporting partners and providing for children. The movement increasingly attracted people who understood the personal and political actions needed to address the racism, sexism, classism, and heterosexism that oppressed black women. As new organizations flourished in the late 1970s and early 1980s, the Black Feminist Movement's ideals and themes grew more inclusive. According to Barbara Smith's introduction to *Home Girls: A Black Feminist Anthology*:

> *Reproductive rights, sterilization abuse, equal access to abortion, health care, child care, the rights of the disabled, violence against women, rape, battery, sexual harassment, welfare rights, lesbian and gay rights, aging, police brutality, labor organizing, anti-imperialist struggles, anti-racist organizing, nuclear disarmament, and preserving the environment.*

The Combahee River Collective broke new ground with work that was expressly socialist and actively promoted the acceptance of sisterhood among black women of all sexual orientations. Black lesbians such as Audre Lorde, Pat Parker, Margaret Sloan, and Barbara Smith were the vanguard of the Black Feminist Movement. The 1973 founding Combahee River Collective Statement stated:

> *The most general statement of our politics at the present time would be that we are actively committed to struggling against racial, sexual, heterosexual, and class oppression, and see as our particular task the development of integrated analysis and practice based upon the fact that the major systems of oppression are interlocking. The synthesis of these oppressions creates the conditions of our lives. As Black women we see Black feminism as the logical political movement to combat the manifold and simultaneous oppression that all women of color face.*

This is now a key document in the history of the Black Feminist Movement.

The movement succeeded in creating a cross-class coalition of black women from all walks of life. The theory created by black feminist writers and the activism across the nations forced the inclusion of their texts and theories in traditionally all-white women's studies courses on campuses across the country. Black feminists faced many limitations and challenges, including the need to connect to non-Western women of color movements around the world while finding ways to engage black men for the liberation of all black people.

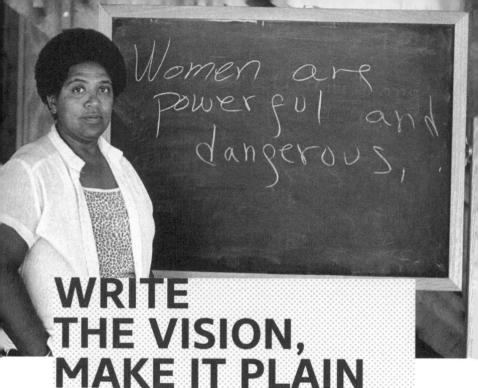

Women are powerful and dangerous,

WRITE THE VISION, MAKE IT PLAIN

BLACK WOMEN TALK BLACK FEMINISM

Having formed a movement of their own, black feminists began to determine and define goals for themselves. Most notable is author Alice Walker's definition, coining the term "Womanism," to describe the Black Feminist Movement:

Above: Writer, poet and activist Audre Lorde lectures students at the Atlantic Center for the Arts in New Smyrna Beach, Florida, in 1983.

*Womanist. 1. From womanish (opp. of "girlish,"
i.e., frivolous, irresponsible, not serious). A
black feminist or feminist of color. Usually
referring to outrageous, audacious, courageous
or willful behavior. Wanting to know more and
in greater depth than is considered "good" for
one. Responsible. In charge. Serious. 2. Also: A
woman who loves other women, sexually and/or
non-sexually. Appreciates and prefers women's
culture, women's emotional flexibility (values
tears as natural counterbalance of laughter), and
women's strength. Committed to the survival
and wholeness of entire people, male and female.
Not separatist, except periodically, for health.*

The Black Feminist aesthetic was crafted, and the movement created, in the hands of writers.

Black Feminist thought included ideas produced by black women for black women. Based on an assessment of the sociopolitical and historical context of black women's lives in the United States, these ideas signified that only black women could articulate their perspectives as they reflected on their experiences. The role of writers and academics was to document these standpoints for black women in all levels of social strata. A tension began for black women within academia, which insisted on the use of

DID YOU KNOW

Alice Walker was the first African American to win the Pulitzer Prize for Literature as well as the National Book Award in 1983 for her novel *The Color Purple*. The book was adapted into a film in 1985 by Steven Spielberg.

The Black Woman, *edited by Toni Cade Bambara, is the first major creative Black Feminist anthology of the period. It features works by Jean Bond, Nikki Giovanni, Abbey Lincoln, Audre Lorde, Paule Marshall, Gwen Patton, Pat Robinson, Alice Walker, and Shirley Williams.*

standard English for publications when many black feminist scholars used the language and dialect of the people and their students to articulate theories in support of black female self-representation. Two of the most prominent black feminist writers from the movement are Alice Walker and Audre Lorde, whose literary production and social activism have framed the contours of the black feminist movement and its literature.

ALICE WALKER (Alice Malsenior Walker) was born on February 9, 1944, in Eatonton, Georgia. An internationally celebrated author and activist, her roots are deeply grounded in the Civil Rights and Black Liberation movements of the 1950s and 1960s. Her emergence as a central voice in the Black Feminist Movement came when she defined "womanism" as the work that black feminists were engaged in during the 1970s. As a child of sharecropper parents, Walker was accidently injured in the eye by a BB gun, shot by her brother. Her partial blindness led her to withdraw socially, and she began writing poetry as a creative outlet for coping with the isolation caused by the injury. Walker was active in the Civil Rights movement, especially in voter registration drives in Georgia. After earning a Bachelor of Arts from Sarah Lawrence College in 1965, Walker began the difficult work of balancing life as an activist, mother, partner, writer, and academic. An analysis of Walker's writing states that she:

> Describes the emotional, spiritual, and physical devastation that occurs when family trust is betrayed. Her focus is on African-American women, who live in a larger world and struggle to achieve independent identities beyond male domination. . . . Walker's stories focus not so much on the racial violence that occurs among strangers, but the violence among friends and family members, a kind of deliberate cruelty.

Author of seven novels, four collections of short stories, four childrens books, and collections of poetry and essays, Walker is also also credited with rediscovering and championing Harlem Renaissance writer Zora Neale Hurston.

ZORA NEALE HURSTON is one of the preeminent writers of 20th-century African-American literature. Hurston was the first African-American graduate of Barnard College and was the author of four novels, her most famous being *Their Eyes Were Watching God*. She also wrote two books on folklore from her training as a cultural anthropologist. She died in obscurity and was buried in an unmarked grave in Florida until Alice Walker became interested in her work and decided to find her gravesite. This moment of serendipity was documented in an article by Walker titled "Looking for Zora," published by *Ms.* magazine in 1975 and reprinted in Walker's essay collection *In Search of Our Mother's Gardens* in 1983. Walker, pretending to be Hurston's niece, trudged through waist-high grass in the cemetery while calling Zora's name. Sinking into an unmarked gravesite, Walker found Hurston's final resting place and quickly installed a proper headstone. It is with the momentum of this find that Walker began discussing Hurston's legacy in classrooms and conferences across the United States. All of Hurston's books were reprinted, and today *Their Eyes Were Watching God* is one of the most read books in American literature.

AUDRE LORDE was a poet, novelist, and activist born on February 18, 1934, in New York to Grenadian parents. She received her Bachelor of Arts from Hunter College of the City University of New York and and a Master of Library Science from Columbia University. She was a librarian in New York for seven years, and published several volumes of poetry between 1968 and 1986. Writing as a lesbian, a mother, and a daughter, her poems are committed to envisioning a life where women of all sexual orientations are accepted and can work as allies for social change. Diagnosed with breast cancer in 1980, Lorde chronicled her fight for survival in *The Cancer Journals*, which won the Gay Caucus Book of the Year in 1981. Her other prose includes *Zami: A New Spelling of my Name* (1982), *Sister Outsider: Essays and Speeches* (1984), and *A Burst of Light* (1988), which won a National Book Award.

Lorde's words created a new space where women of color could embrace their sexuality and find affirmation in their bodies and personal choices while never compromising their political integrity. Lorde's compassionate search for justice also

[
Black Feminist Thought, by Patricia Hill Collins, explores the work of Black Feminist scholars, including Angela Davis, bell hooks, Alice Walker, and Audre Lorde.
]

brought black men to an understanding of the black feminist movement. In partnership with Barbara Smith, Lorde founded Kitchen Table: Women of Color Press in the 1980s. She was also a founding member of Sisters in Support of Sisters in South Africa, which raised awareness of the oppression that black South African women experienced under apartheid. Poet laureate of New York State from 1991 to 1992, Lorde succumbed to breast cancer in 1992.

IN PLAIN SIGHT

AFRICAN-AMERICAN ARTISTS CHALLENGE INJUSTICE

Many African-American artists have expressed their visions and voices on stage, on screen, in song, and on canvas. Visual artists have inscribed the searing beauty of African-American life for the world to see, seeking ways to use art as activism. All of these artists have an African-American aesthetic in their art, serving as inspiration for other artists, historians, educators, and social movements. These 10 artists are a highlight of prominent African-American individuals who have committed their creative vision to documenting history and making black life visible in America.

ROMARE BEARDEN (1911–1988), the first art director of the Harlem Cultural Council in 1964, is celebrated for his richly textured collages documenting the intricacies of African-American life, especially jazz.

ELIZABETH CATLETT'S (1915–2012) life-size wooden sculptures celebrate the endurance of African-American women in the liberation struggle.

SAMELLA LEWIS (born 1924), visual artist, art historian, and African-American art custodian, has created art for the canvas while serving as a repository for African-American artistic production.

JACOB LAWRENCE (1917–2000) used his paintings to document historical aspects of African-American life, and is best known for his "Migration Series."

KARA WALKER (born 1969) is known for her provocative black paper cut-outs exposing the underbelly of U.S. plantation slavery.

MICKALENE THOMAS (born 1971) is a contemporary African-American artist who explores black female beauty in her signature collage-inspired paintings.

KEHINDE WILEY (born 1977) is celebrated for his beyond-life-size paintings of black and brown people disrupting history and visibility.

HANK WILLIS THOMAS (born 1976) uses his photography to challenge the ways black bodies are represented, especially by corporate America.

JAVAKA STEPTOE (born 1971) is an award-winning African-American children's book writer and illustrator.

RENEE COX (born 1960), one of the most controversial African-American artists today, uses her body (sometimes nude) to resist stereotypical notions of representing black womanhood.

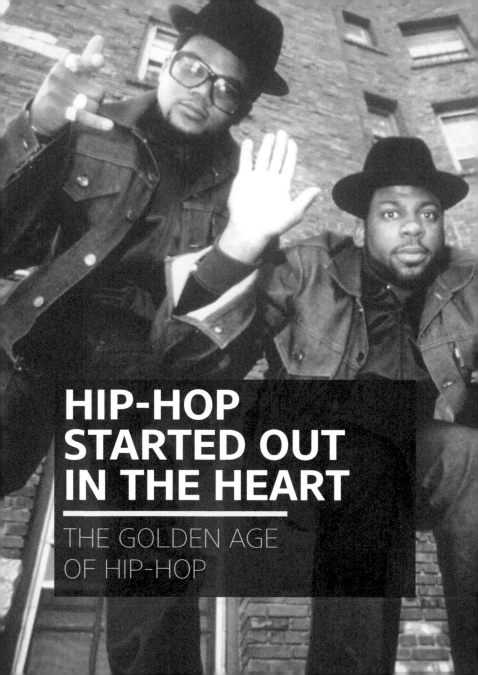

HIP-HOP STARTED OUT IN THE HEART

THE GOLDEN AGE
OF HIP-HOP

Hip-hop, as a cultural form of expression starting in the 1970s with DJ Kool Herc in the Bronx, grappled with its political identity by the late 1980s as it moved into mainstream culture. Becoming more than a form of entertainment, it emerged as a viable social tool to reflect on urban ills. Hip-hop reached its peak of sociopolitical expression with the establishment of Native Tongues in 1988. With NWA's (Niggaz Wit Attitudes) 1988 release of their gangsta rap album *Straight Outta Compton*, the tide changed forever. Identity as a hardcore gangsta rapper was articulated by the valorization of

Run DMC in New York.

acquiring women, drinking, gambling, and posturing, moving the genre away from social consciousness The lines dividing East Coast and West Coast rap were permanently etched when New York–based Jungle Brothers released *Straight Out the Jungle*, an Afro-centric album focusing on the difficulties of black urban living.

NATIVE TONGUES

The Native Tongues collective was established in 1988. The debut albums of its founding members (The Jungle Brothers' *Straight out the Jungle*, De La Soul's *3 Feet High and Rising*, and Tribe's *People's Instinctive Travels and the Paths of Rhythm*) were a combination of innovative styles based in African-American jazz traditions, highly conscious critiques of American life, and pure entertainment. Native Tongues members were affiliated with Afrika Bambaataa's Universal Zulu Nation, an organization promoting unity and culture through hip-hop, as its ideas on Afro-centrism resonated with Native Tongue's musical production. Core members of Native Tongues included A Tribe Called Quest (Q-Tip, Phife Dawg, Ali Shaheed Muhammad, and Jarobi White, with a guest appearance by Consquence in 1996); De La Soul (Posdnuos, Trugoy, and Maseo); Jungle Brothers (Mike Gee, Afrika Baby Bam, and DJ Sammy B); Monie Love; Queen Latifah;

Black Sheep (Dres and Mista Lawnge); and Chi-Ali.

Welcomed into the Native Tongues collective, Queen Latifah released her debut album, *All Hail the Queen*, in 1989. A decidedly Afro-centric and socially conscious record, Latifah's music made clear her commitment to black feminism, a new topic for what began as a boys' club; She used hip-hop as a tool for activism and consciousness-raising, nationally and internationally, along with other members of Native Tongues.

Continuing the Native Tongues' tradition of fostering new talent, black British artist Monie Love was featured on Queen Latifah's song "Ladies First." Love went on to release her own album, *Down to Earth*. The inclusion of both these artists in the Native Tongues collective was an important step for hip-hop as it marked a move away from the patriarchal tendencies of the Black Liberation struggles of the 1970s.

By 1993, Native Tongues drifted apart as the founders began producing music with different ideological directions. However, the path had been carved, and many new-generation artists (including Mos Def, Talib Kweli, and J Dilla)

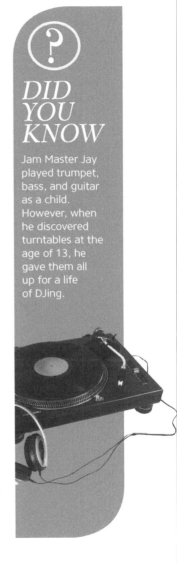

DID YOU KNOW

Jam Master Jay played trumpet, bass, and guitar as a child. However, when he discovered turntables at the age of 13, he gave them all up for a life of DJing.

took up the mantle and created work that inspired another Native Tongues–like collective in 2000, called the Soulquarians, which included Common, Questlove, Erykah Badu, and other influential artists. Native Tongues' influence is heard in the contemporary music of Pharrell, Kanye West, and Kendrick Lamar, among others.

WU-TANG CLAN

In 1993, Wu-Tang Clan (comprised of Cappadonna, Ghostface Killah, GZA/Genuis, Inspectah Deck, Masta Killa, Method Man, Ol' Dirty Bastard, Raekwon, RZA, and U-God) became the most revolutionary rap group of the 1990s. Their debut album, *Enter the Wu-Tang (36 Chambers)*, in 1993, was part of an innovative business plan that allowed each group member to be free agents

HIP-HOP'S INFLUENCE ON POP CULTURE

1989
Method Man from the Wu-Tang Clan was an actor on the television show *The Wire*

2008

Inspired by rapper MC Hammer, harem pants are now in vogue in the fashion world

Will Smith and Jazzy Jeff receive the first Grammy ever given to hip-hop artists

2003

Hilary Clinton is endorsed by 50 Cent and Timbaland

2012

while releasing music under the Wu-Tang name. They garnered tremendous success individually and collectively.

DIGABLE PLANETS

New York–based trio Digable Planets quickly gained an audience that was underwhelmed by the hyper-aggressiveness of gangsta rap, which was flooding the airwaves at the time. Ladybug Mecca stood out as the group's female lyricist; she helped the group produce music that redefined hip-hop. Combining poetry, funk, samba, jazz, and inventive arrangements, Digable Planets made clear that they were deeply influenced by African-American jazz greats. Sophisticated in their language, Digable Planet's references ranged from Karl Marx and bell hooks to Nikki Giovanni. They were conscious and cool, and they had a new artistic sound.

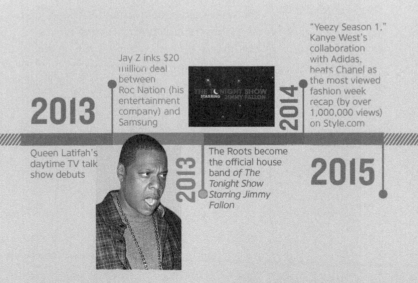

2013 Jay Z inks $20 million deal between Roc Nation (his entertainment company) and Samsung

2014 "Yeezy Season 1," Kanye West's collaboration with Adidas, beats Chanel as the most viewed fashion week recap (by over 1,000,000 views) on Style.com

Queen Latifah's daytime TV talk show debuts

2013 The Roots become the official house band *of The Tonight Show Starring Jimmy Fallon*

2015

QUEEN LATIFAH

"Ladies First," by Queen Latifah, placed African-American hip-hop artists in direct conversation with the anti-apartheid movement in South Africa.

THE FUGEES

The Fugees was a hip-hop trio that gained prominence in the mid-1990s for its social consciousness. The members of the group, Wyclef Jean, Lauryn Hill, and Pras Michel, combined hip-hop with soul and reggae, which was a first. In 1997 The Fugees won two Grammys, one for Best R&B Vocal Performance by a Duo or Group for "Killing Me Softly," and Best Rap Album for *The Score*. Before dissolving in late 1997, they recorded three albums together: *Blunted on Reality* (1994), *The Score* (1996), and *Bootleg Versions* (1996). Their multi-platinum albums were deeply rooted in global consciousness, and they voiced support for oppressed people around world as well as within their own African-American communities.

BOOMERANG
GHOSTS OF
A VIOLENT
PAST

SOCIAL JUSTICE AND
PROTECTING THE LIVES OF
AFRICAN–AMERICAN MEN

While hip-hop artists used their words to express disdain for the economic and social crisis facing urban black America, everyday citizens joined their voices together in protest on the streets of the United States in the 1990s.

In March 1991, Rodney King and two others were driving on I-210 through Los Angeles. Ordered by California Highway Patrol officers to stop, King did not, leading to a high-speed chase. Finally stopping and exiting the car, King was brutally beaten by the police in what they say was an "attempt to subdue"

DID YOU KNOW

Former New York City Mayor David Dinkins and Congressman Charles Rangel were arrested for protesting the acquittal of the officers in the Diallo murder. Other arrests included Ossie Davis, Ruby Dee, and Dick Gregory, as African-American celebrities added their voices to the protests.

No Justice!
No Peace!
Amadou Diallo

him. The entire beating was recorded on videotape by a local resident. On April 29, 1992, after seven days of deliberation, a mostly white jury acquitted three of the four accused officers, stating that they could not determine if the officers used excessive force. This sparked six days of riots during which thousands of people in Los Angeles protested. More than 53 people were killed and more than 2,000 were injured. Marching the streets in protest against police brutality, even when caught on film, African Americans and their allies decided to hold a rally for peace on the fourth day of the riots, when the Marines and Army were sent in to disperse rioters.

More than 30,000 people attended the demonstration. In April 1993, a federal investigation found two officers guilty of excessive force while two others were acquitted. King was awarded $3.8 million in damages. The legacy of the LA riots was unmistakable, once again bringing police brutality and the biased justice system to the forefront, as well as police relationships with black America.

Amadou Diallo, a Fulani immigrant from Guinea, moved to the Bronx in 1997. He sold gloves, socks, and other odds and ends on the street, sending most of his money back home to help his family. He was brutally murdered on February 4, 1999, by four plainclothes police officers from the aggressive Street Crimes Unit as he entered his apartment building. They shot 41 times, with 19 bullets hitting his body, although Diallo was unarmed. The four white officers each carried 9 millimeter semi-automatic service pistols that hold 16 bullets and can be discharged in seconds—although the officers were trained by a department that taught officers never to use their weapons unless they have no other recourse. The officers stated that they approached Diallo because he fit the description of a person of interest. When Diallo reached for his wallet to present ID, the officers thought he was pulling a gun and shot him. The officers faced prosecution on second-degree murder but were acquitted by a jury in Albany.

Most interesting during the trial were the officers' own testimonies. The officers admitted that they never pictured the scene from Diallo's perspective. From Diallo's view, he must have been terrified, as he was in the vestibule of his apartment building watching four white men, armed with guns approaching him. Trying to blame Diallo for his own death, the officers claimed that he would not listen to their commands and did not keep his hands in sight. As he was digging in his pocket for identification, the officers did not give him the benefit of the doubt, and didn't recognize that as an African immigrant, he may not speak English with enough proficiency to understand their directives and respond properly. Though the officers acknowledged that they made a lethal mistake, Diallo still lost his life over mistaken identity and a communication breakdown that could have been avoided.

LIKES AND HASHTAGS

SOCIAL MEDIA DECIDES WHO SPEAKS

I n the 21st century, social media has revolutionized movements for social change as the most meaningful and mobilizing platform for political progress, information-sharing, global critiques, and support.

Facebook, Twitter, Instagram, Reddit, and Tumblr connect much of the planet. Blogs, e-zines, and online businesses are maintained daily as millions of people write, read, critique, post pictures, and garner attention to topics on their corners of the world. From Barack Obama's "Yes We Can" 2008 presidential campaign slogan to the Arab Spring movements in Tunisia, Egypt, Libya, and Yemen, social media's presence has fostered worldwide awareness that connects people, especially youth, in unprecedented ways, creating dialogue through powerful political messaging and peer-to-peer public conversation.

Twitter has transformed political activism by empowering people to broadcast their second-by-second experiences. It has become a critical tool for accessing and sharing instant information about the news, politics, and police brutality. Since the 2012 murder of Trayvon Martin, an unarmed African-American teen killed by George Zimmerman, who was later acquitted, the instantaneous information sharing and grassroots organizing has mushroomed, thanks to Twitter and other social media platforms as launching pads for political movements.

According to media psychologist Dr. Pamela Rutledge:

The 2008 Obama presidential campaign made history. Not only was Obama the first African American to be elected president, but he was also the first presidential candidate to effectively use social media as a major campaign strategy. . . . [Today], 66 percent of social media users actively engage in political activism online. . . . Obama is the first "social media president." In the 2012 campaign, Obama logged twice as many Facebook "likes" and nearly 20 times as many re-tweets as his Republican challenger, Mitt Romney.

Obama's team understood the power of social media to spread content and consciousness through personal engagement and follow-through. Using social media in 2008, the Obama team encouraged small donations easily sent via cellphone apps, rather than only courting large donors. The first digital president, Obama raised nearly $1 billion using social media while mobilizing thousands of volunteers under the #YesWeCan hashtag. Through email, blogs, social networks, and texting, an entire digital community carried in the election of Obama. Benn Rosales, founder of AGbeat.com, notes that Obama's 2008 campaign began as a grassroots cause; Obama "built an entire campaign on the viral nature of pop culture." As supporters turned out for mass rallies, organizers would collect cellphone and email data. By the end of an evening, thank-you messages and a direct link to the Obama campaign page would be in your inbox or sent via text.

As president, Obama and his team have continued using social media to his advantage. On July 6, 2011, he hosted a

"Twitter Presents Town Hall at the White House." Held in the East Room of the White House and streamed online, President Obama gave spoken responses (unrestricted by Twitter's 140 characters) to tweeted questions about the economy and jobs under the hashtag #AskObama.

BLACK TWITTER

Many of Obama's supporters stay engaged through Black Twitter, an online movement comprising African Americans who use Twitter. The earliest mention of Black Twitter appeared in an article, "Black Twitter: A Starter's Kit," published by *The Root* on February 4, 2010. (*The Root* is an online African American cultural magazine founded and edited by Henry Louis Gates Jr.) African Americans use the Black Twitter bird logo as a symbol of communication and identification. Trayvon Martin's death in 2012 spurred an unprecedented social movement on Twitter within black America. Recent hashtag campaigns include #WeAreTrayvonMartin, #APAHeadlines (following the shooting of Renisha McBride), #BlackLivesMatter, and #IfTheyGunMeDown (after the killings of Mike Brown and Eric Garner). Following these hashtags, millions of tweets have shaped discussion, shared rally information, used photographs as historical context for police brutality in the United States, and documented live engagement in civil disobedience.

BLACK LIVES MATTER

#BlackLivesMatter was created in 2013 by Alicia Garza, Patrisse Cullors, and Opal Tometi after Trayvon Martin was shot and

Protestors staged a "die-in" in December 2014, against grand jury decisions from Ferguson, Missouri.

killed. It is a call to action, and a response to the pervasive antiblack racism embedded in American culture. Moving beyond the Civil Rights rhetoric of the 1960s, #BlackLivesMatter:

> *Affirms the lives of black queers and trans folks, disabled folks, black undocumented folks, folks with records, women and all black lives along the gender spectrum. It centers [on] those that have been marginalized within Black Liberation movements. It is a tactic to (re)build the Black Liberation movement. When we say Black Lives Matter, we are broadening the conversation around state violence to include all the ways in which black people are intentionally left powerless at the hands of the state. We are talking about the ways in which black lives are deprived of our basic human rights and dignity.*

Instagram and Facebook are increasingly popular and mobilizing spaces for African Americans—according to a 2012 Pew Research Center report, 23 percent of African Americans use Instagram, and entire social movements have gone viral through Facebook. According to a 2009 Facebook blog report, "Facebook's users are 11 percent African American and saw a surge in adoption in 2009, up from 7 percent in 2005. The African American U.S. population is 12 percent."

On Instagram, Facebook, and Twitter, people worldwide have supported the #BlackLivesMatter movement, from Palestine to Johannesburg. The globe continues to get smaller as people voice stories and connect across communities.

THE TOP 10

WHERE WERE YOU?

1 Montgomery Bus Boycott, December 5, 1955–December 20, 1956, Montgomery, Alabama

2 March on Washington, August 28, 1963, Washington, D.C.

3 Selma to Montgomery March, March 7, 1965, Selma, Alabama

4 The Watts Rebellion, August 11–17, 1965, Los Angeles

8 March and Protest for Trayvon Martin,
June 15, 2013, Los Angeles

9 Ferguson Protest
in Support of Michael Brown, August 2014, Ferguson,Missouri

10 #BlackLivesMatter Protest
Washington Square Park, December 13, 2014, New York

5 Rodney King Protest,
April 29, 1992, Los Angeles

6 Million Man March,
October 16, 1995, Washington, D.C.

7 Million Youth March,
September 5, 1998, New York City

**ANY AND
ALL BLACK
LIVES MATTER**

SUPPORTING BLACK
YOUTH AND THE
LGBT COMMUNITY

Though Bayard Rustin was an openly gay activist and one of the central leaders of the Civil Rights movement, he worked largely behind the scenes because of his sexuality. At one point, Martin Luther King Jr. was persuaded to shift away from Rustin because of homophobic sentiments within the black community. Rustin's double oppression as a gay black man gave him particular insight into the urgency of black liberation. The evolution of the 2013 #BlackLivesMatter movement, with its mission to empower all marginalized black people, especially those in the LGBT community, has has challenged and expanded the ideas behind the earlier Civil Rights movement. It also allowed more visibility and voice for black women in every step of the movement.

By fostering an inclusive community of black Americans from all walks of life, #BlackLivesMatter has opened the door for a new group of activists to join forces in contemporary black liberation struggles; it has become a global symbol for potential social movements on social media as well as on the streets.

ALICIA GARZA is the cofounder of #BlackLivesMatter, and the special projects director for the National Domestic Workers Alliance (NDWA). She has served as executive director of People Organized to Win Employment Rights (POWER) in San Francisco since 2009. The recipient of countless awards, including the San Francisco Local Hero Award and the Jeanne Gauna Communicate Justice Award, Garza has twice been honored by the Harvey Milk Democratic Club with the Bayard Rustin Community Activist award for her community work in San Francisco. Garza is a board member of the School of Unity and Liberation (SOUL) in

Left: Transgendered televison star Laverne Cox was recognized as one of Logo TV's Trailblazers (2014).

Oakland. In discussing the poignancy of the #BlackLivesMatter movement and the importance of "black" in #BlackLivesMatter, Garza stated:

> It is appropriate and necessary to have strategy and action centered on blackness without other non-black communities of color, or white folks for that matter, needing to find a place and a way to center themselves within it. It is appropriate and necessary for us to acknowledge the critical role that black lives and struggles for black liberation have played in inspiring and anchoring, through practice and theory, social movements for liberation of all people. The women's movement, the Chicano liberation movement, queer movements, and many more have adopted the strategies, tactics, and theory of the Black Liberation movement. And if we are committed to a world where all lives matter, we are called to support the very movement that inspired and activated so many more. That means supporting and acknowledging black lives.

PATRISSE CULLORS is an artist, organizer, activist, and cofounder of #BlackLivesMatter. Based in Los Angeles, she has spent the last 17 years working as an artist. Her art is a reflection of her life as a "working class queer, black, cis-gender female to draw forth the way societal norms share her and her communities lives, and produces word that illuminates and highlights racism, classism, homophobia, and trans-phobia." She has worked incessantly to promote law-enforcement accountability across the United States. As the founder of Dignity and Power Now, Cullors works to protect incarcerated people and their families in Los Angeles. As part of her work with #BlackLivesMatter, Cullors was on the frontlines in the streets of Ferguson and St. Louis. She brought more than 500 people from around the nation

[
TRANS activists took to city hall in San Francisco, working under the hashtag #TurnUp4TransPeople, to bring light to recent murders of five trans women (Penny Proud, Ty Underwood, Lamia Beard, Yazmin Vash Payne, and Taja DeJesus) and the disproportionate abuse faced by trans women.
]

to participate in the "Freedom Ride" from St. Louis to Ferguson.

OPAL TOMETI is the executive director of the Black Alliance for Just Immigration and a cofounder of #BlackLivesMatter. Called by *Essence* magazine in October 2014 a new civil rights leader, Tometi's dedication to just immigration in the United States is drawn from personal experience. Born in Phoenix, to Nigerian immigrant parents, Tometi struggled with the deportations of friends and family throughout her childhood. In order to find answers to the disappearance of loved ones, she began researching anti-immigration initiatives and their resemblance to Jim Crow laws. Worried that the civil rights gains of the 1960s will vanish based on anti-immigration laws in the United States, Tometi stated:

DID YOU KNOW

Laverne Cox is the first trans woman of color to have a leading role on a mainstream scripted television show. Cox is also the first trans woman of color to produce and star in her own television show, VH1's TRANSForm, which was nominated for a GLAAD Media Award.

Activist Art McCoy holds a photo of Tamir Rice before a protest march at Cudell Park in Cleveland, Monday, Nov. 24, 2014.

As the global economy becomes more dire, we see more black people from the diaspora brave the U.S. borders looking for what they think will be better terrain. What people often find are hard conditions, relentless discrimination, and criminalization.

WHAT ABOUT THE CHILDREN?

One of the recent cases that has drawn support from #Black-LivesMatter is the killing of 12-year-old Tamir Rice. On November 22, 2014, in Cleveland, Ohio, two white police officers, Timothy Loehmann and Frank Garmback, responded to a dispatch call about "a male sitting on a swing pointing a gun at people in a city park." The police were told at least twice that the gun was probably fake and that the male was still a child. When the police arrived on the scene, they found 12-year-old Tamir in the park. Told to put his hands up, Tamir allegedly reached toward the toy gun, an Airsoft replica, that shot orange plastic pellets. Officer Loehmann fired two shots within two seconds of exiting the car, hitting Rice in the chest. There was no time for warnings; the officers just reacted, and a child was senselessly killed. The shooting was recorded by a surveillance camera across the street that clearly showed Rice's innocence and the reckless behavior of the Cleveland police. Attempting to blame Rice for his own death, the Cleveland police maintained that the officers could not distinguish if Rice's gun was real or fake. The city of Cleveland turned the investigation over to the Cuyahoga County Sheriff's Department, which ruled the shooting a homicide.

TRENDING
TOPICS
CELEBS
SPEAK BACK

AFRICAN AMERICANS
BREAKING BARRIERS

Facing a pessimistic time in history when police brutality, antiblack sentiment, and racism are rampant, many African Americans look to celebrities and athletes to take a stand, as John Carlos and Tommie Smith did at the 1968 Olympics, relying on their respected international platforms for support.

Usher, Kobe Bryant, Beyoncé, Jay Z, LeBron James, Chris Brown, Samuel L. Jackson, and Dave Chappelle are a few of the celebrities who have raised awareness for various movements, including #BlackLivesMatter, #HandsUpDontShoot, and #ICantBreathe. Samuel L. Jackson posted a video of him singing "We Ain't Gonna Stop, Til People are Free," written by the Bronx's Peace Poets, on his Facebook page, along with a challenge to other celebrities who took the Ice Bucket Challenge (the ALS Challenge of dumping ice water on your head to promote awareness of Lou Gehrig's Disease), to also sing the following:

I can hear my neighbor crying, I can't breathe
Now I'm in the struggle and I can't leave
Calling out the violence of the racist police
We aint gonna stop til people are free
We aint gonna stop til people are free.

With more than a million views, Jackson's page was filled with supporter videos; this contemporary protest song has become a chant at rallies and demonstrations all over the United States.

Cleveland Browns wide receiver Andrew Hawkins publicly defended wearing a T-shirt at pregame warm-ups that read "Justice for Tamir Rice and John Crawford." On the back it read "The Real Battle for Ohio." Cleveland Police Union President Jeff Follmer called Hawkins's shirt "pathetic" and advised that he should not get politically involved; he should simply do his job as an athlete. Hawkins stated that wearing the T-shirt "wasn't a stance against every police officer or every police department. My wearing of the T-shirt was a stance against wrong individuals doing the wrong thing for the wrong reason to innocent people."

Cleveland Cavaliers superstars LeBron James and Kyrie Irving wore "I Can't Breathe" T-shirts while warming up for a December 2014 game against the Brooklyn Nets. The Nets' Jarret Jack, Alan Anderson, Deron Williams, and Kevin Garnett also wore the T-shirts. "I Can't Breathe" were the final words spoken by New Yorker Eric Garner in July 2014 as he was killed in a chokehold executed illegally by a New York City police officer.

A WORD ABOUT

Hip-hop mogul and Def Jam cofounder Russell Simmons has been very active in the #BlackLivesMatter movement. Simmons and Jay Z met with New York Governor Andrew Cuomo on December 10, 2014, to discuss criminal justice reforms in the wake of Eric Garner's and Michael Brown's deaths.

Considered the royal couple of the entertainment industry, Beyoncé and Jay Z joined the "Justice for Trayvon Martin" vigil in Manhattan on July 20, 2014, a week after the acquittal of George Zimmerman. They greeted Sybrina Fulton, Trayvon's mother, and the Reverend Al Sharpton, who organized the vigil. The day before at his "Legends of the Summer" concert at Yankee Stadium with Justin Timberlake, Jay Z dedicated the song "Forever Young" to Trayvon. Al Sharpton quoted Jay Z, who did not want to speak to the crowd of thousands, as saying, "We all feel the pain and apprehension—the laws must protect everybody or it doesn't protect anybody. We do not come from hate; we come from love of children."

Beyoncé, in her own form of activism, tweeted #actnow4Trayvon on July 19, 2014, and attached a link asking for fans to sign a MoveOn.org petition. On her Tumblr account, Beyoncé stated, "Trayvon Martin's most basic civil right, the right to live, was violated." She also asked for a moment of silence at her Miami concert following Zimmerman's acquittal.

Solange Knowles, songwriter, DJ, creative director of Puma, and sister of Beyoncé Knowles, staged a peaceful

Jay Z and Beyoncé attend a 2013 rally in New York protesting the jury's decision finding George Zimmerman not guilty of shooting Trayvon Martin.

protest in Brooklyn, where she spoke in front of a crowd of hundreds. On her Twitter account she wrote, "Seeing & gathering with people today/tonight all for the same fight helped to restore my faith in humanity."

At the 2015 Grammy Awards, during his performance of "Happy," Pharrell led a "Hand's Up, Don't Shoot" chant, paying homage to 18-year-old Michael Brown, killed by police officer Darren Wilson in Ferguson, Missouri. With his backup dancers wearing black hoodies, Pharrell also paid homage to Trayvon Martin. That same night, when Beyoncé performed "Precious Lord Take My Hand," written by Thomas Dorsey, from the movie *Selma*, the all-male choir behind her raised their hands in the "Hands Up, Don't Shoot" pose.

A PARTING
THOUGHT

"There is really nothing more to say-except why?
But since why is difficult to handle,
one must take refuge in how."

—TONI MORRISON, *THE BLUEST EYE*

BIBLIOGRAPHY

Aalbc.com. "Larry Neal." Accessed March 20, 2015. www.aalbc.com/authors/larry.htm.

AceShowbiz.com. "The Fugees Awards." Accessed March 24, 2015. www.aceshowbiz.com/celebrity/the_fugees/awards.html.

Adaso, Henry. "A Brief History of Hip-Hop." About Entertainment. Accessed March 13, 2015. www.rap.about.com/od/rootsofraphiphop/p/RootsOfRap.

AfroCubaWeb. "Assata Shakur." Accessed March 19, 2015. www.afrocubaweb.assata.

American Rhetoric: Online Speech Bank. "Martin Luther King, Jr.: 'Beyond Vietnam- A Time to Break Silence.'" April 4, 1967. Accessed March 13, 2015. www.americanrhetoric.com/speeches/mlktimestobreaksilence.

Anderson, Stacy. "Study Digs into African American Use of Twitter and Technology."

Huffington Post Black Voices. January 7, 2014. Accessed March 25, 2015. www.huffingtonpost.com/2014/01/07/black-twitter-technology-n-4554062.

Armstrong, Lisa. "*Essence* Magazine: The New Civil Rights Leaders." Black Alliance for Just Immigration. October 10, 2014. Accessed March 25, 2015. www.blackalliance.org/essence-magazine-the-new-civil-rights-leaders.

Art Makers. "Sonia Sanchez." Accessed March 20, 2015. www.thehistorymakers.com/biography/sonia-sanchez-39.

Artspace. "Mikalene Thomas." Accessed March 23, 2015. www.artspace.com/michalene_thomas.

B20. "Number of African-Americans on Facebook Mirrors US Makeup." December 17, 2009.Accessed March 25, 2015. www.blackweb20.com/2009/12/17/number-of-african-americans-on-facebook-mirrors-us-makeup.

Baker, Debbi. "Samuel Jackson wants 'Ice Bucket Challenge' Celebs to Sing Police Protest Song." UT San Diego. December 15, 2014. Accessed March 25, 2015. www.utsandiego.com/news/2014/dec/15/samuel-jackson-cant-breathe-song-challenge

Baraka, Amiri "Amiri Baraka: Poet, Playwright, Activist." Accessed March 20, 2015. www.amiribaraka.com.

BET. "Celebs in the Civil Rights Movement." Accessed March 14, 2015. www.bet.com/celebrities/photos/celebs-in -the-civil-rights-movement.

Binns, Lisa. "Harry Belafonte: My Mission is Near Its End." March 2, 2015. Al Jazeera America. Accessed March 16, 2015. www.america.aljazeera. com/watch/shows/america-tonight/articles/2015/3/2/ harry-belafonte-my-mission-is-near-its-end.

Biography.com. "Arthur Ashe." Accessed March 10, 2015. www.biography. com/people/arthurashe9190544.

Biography.com. "Marcus Garvey." Accessed March 13, 2015. www.biography.com/people/marcus-garvey-93073.

Biography.com. "Michael Jordan." Accessed March 11, 2015. www.biography.com/people/michael-jordan-935806.

Biography.com. "Paul Robeson." Accessed March 13, 2015. www.biography. com/people/paul-robesonn-946041.

Biography.com. "Toni Morrison." Accessed March 10, 2015. www.biography.com/people/toni-morrison-9415590#branching-out.

Biography.com. "Ralph Bunche." Accessed May 8, 2015. http://www.biography.com/people/ralph-bunche-9231128

Biography.com. "Hiram R. Revels." Accessed May 8, 2015. http://www. biography.com/people/hiram-r-revels-9456129

Black Lives Matter. "Black Lives Matter." Accessed March 25, 2015. www.blacklivesmatter.come/about.

Blackman, Dexter. "African Americans, Pan-Africanism, and the Anti-Apartheid Campaign to Expel South Africa from the 1968 Olympics." *The Journal of Pan African Studies*, 5(3): 2013.

BlackPast.org. "Watts Rebellion (August 1965)." Accessed March 23, 2015. www.blackpast.org/aaw/watts-rebellion-august-1965.

Blake, John. "Malcolm and Martin, Closer than We Ever Thought." CNN. May, 2010. Accessed March 16, 2015. www.edition.cnn/2010/ LIVING/05/19/Malcolmx.king/index.

Box Office Mojo. "Selma." Accessed March 23, 2015.www.boxofficemojo. com/movies/?page=daily&id=selma.

Boyd, Valerie. "About Zora Neale Hurston." Zora Neale Hurston. Accessed March 20, 2015. www.zoranealehurston.com/about/.

Brunner, Borgna and Haney, Elissa. "Civil Rights Timeline." Infoplease. Accessed March 23, 2015. www.infoplease.com/spot/ civilrightstimeline.1.

Brunner, Borgna. "The Murders of James Chaney, Andrew Goodman, and Michael Schwener." Infoplease.com. Accessed March 16, 2015. www.infoplease.com/spot/bhmjustice4.

Carbone, Nick. "Twitter Town Hall Won't Limit President Obama's Answers." Time. July 2, 2011. Accessed March 25, 2015. www.newsfeed.time.com/2011/07/02/twitter-town-hall-wont-limit-president-obamas-answers.

Carson, Clayborne. "Biography of Martin Luther King, Jr." MLK.online. Accessed March 16, 2015. www.mlkonline.net/bio.

Carter, Kelley. "Meet Black Hollywood's Behind the Scenes Power Players." Ebony. February 6, 2013. Accessed March 25, 2015. www.ebony.com/entertainment-culture/blackhollywoods-behind-the-scenes-power-players-311#axzz3VSI4rKeP.

Chandler, D. "Rodney King Riots in Los Angles Began on This Day in 1992." NewsOnline for Black America. Accessed March 23, 2015. www.newsone.com/2423835/rodney-kingriots-2.

Classic Motown. "The Story of Motown Records." Accessed March 10, 2015. www.classic.motown.com/history/.

CNN. "Black Lives Matter Protests." Accessed March 23, 2015. www.cnn.com.2014/12//13/us/gallery/black-lives-matter-protests/index.

Cochran, Sylvia. "Civil Rights Heroes – Jackie Robinson." Bella Online. Accessed March 16, 2015. www.bellaonline.com/articles/art48766.asp.

Cone, James. Martin & Malcolm & America: A Dream or a Nightmare. New York: OrbisBooks, 1992.

Cooper, Michael. "Officers in Bronx Fire 41 Shots, and an Unarmed man is Killed." New York Times. February 5, 1999. Accessed March 24, 2015. www.nytimes.com/1999/02/05/nyregion/officers-in-bronx-fire-41-shots-and-an-unarmedman-is-killed.

Coyne, John. "Tamir Rice, Boy Shot Dead by Cleveland Police, Did Not Point Replica Gun at Officer." HuffPost. November 24, 2015. Accessed March 25, 2015. Danto, Erzulie.

Democracy Now. "Thousands Protest Acquittal of Police Officers Who Killed Amadou Diallo." February 28, 2000. Accessed March 24, 2015. www.democracynow.org/2000/2/28/thousands-protest-acquittal-of-police-officers.

Discogs. "Digable Planets." Accessed March 24, 2015. www.discogs.com/artist/48393-DigablePlanets.

Duggan, Maeve and Brenner, Joanna. "The Demographics of Social Media Users – 2012." Pew Research Center. February 12, 2012. Accessed March 25, 2015.

Dockterman, Eliana. "Selma Cast and Crew Wear 'I Can't Breathe' Shirts to New York Premiere. Time. December 15, 2014. Accessed March 25, 2015.www.com.3633484/selma-movie-i-cant-breathe-shirts. www.pewinterest.org/files/oldmedia/Files/Reports/2013/PIP_Social-MediaUsers.

Duncan, Garrett Albert. "Black Panther Party." Britianica.com. Accessed March 18, 2015. www.briticannica.com/EBchecked/topic/68134/Black-Panther-Party.

Encyclopedia Britannica. "Black Arts Repertory Theatre." Accessed March 17, 2015. www.britannica.com/EBchecked/topic/67621/Black-Arts-Repertory-Theatre.

Encyclopedia.com. "Black Power Movement." Accessed March 13, 2015. www.encyclopedia.com/topic/Black_Power-movement/aspx.

Encyclopedia of World Biography. "Alice Walker Biography." Accessed March 20, 2015. www.notablebiographies.com/Tu-We/Walker-Alice.

Esaak, Shelley. "Jacob Lawrence Biography." About Education. Accessed March 23, 2015. www.arthistory.about.com/cs/namesll/p/lawrence_j.

Fritsch, Jane. "The Diallo Verdict: The Overview; 4 Officers In Diallo Shooting are Acquitted of all Charges." *New York Times*. February 25, 2000. Accessed March 24, 2015.

Gambino, Lauren. "Eric Garner: grand jury declines to indict NYPD officer over chokehold death." *The Guardian*. December 3, 2014. Accessed March 11, 2015. www.theguardian.com/us-news/2014/dec/03/eric-garner-grand-jury-declines-indict-nypd-chokehold-death.

Garza, Alicia. "A Herstory of the #BlackLivesMatter Movement by Alicia Garza." FeministWire. October 7, 2014. Accessed March 25, 2015. www.thefeministwire.com/2014/10/blacklivesmatter-2.

Giambusso, David. "Amiri Baraka, former N.J, Poet Laureate and Prolific Author, Dead at 79." America's Black Holocaust Museum. Jan 9, 2014. Accessed March 11, 2015. www.abhmuesum.org/2014/amiri-baraka-former-n-j-poet-laureate-and-prolific-author-dead-at-79.

Gonzales, Michael. "Vintage Visions: Baraka and the Black Arts Movement." *Ebony*. January 10, 2014. Accessed March 20, 2015. www. ebony.com/entertainment-culture/on-baraka-and-the-black-arts-movement-111#axzz3Uwil1aoM.

Gordon, Jeremy. "Jay Z, Russell Simmons Meet with New York Governor Andrew Cuomo to Discuss Justice Reforms." Pitchfork. December 11, 2014. Accessed March 25, 2015. www.pitchfork.com/news/57803-jay-z-russel-simmons-meet-with-new-york-governorandrew-cuomo-to-discuss-justice-reforms.

Grammy.org. "Beyoncé." Accessed March 11, 2015. www.grammy.com/artist/beyonce.

Harrison, Lilly. "Beyoncé and Jay Z Attend Trayvon Martin Rally in NYC." ENews. July 21, 2013. Accessed March 25, 2015. www.eonline/news/441067/beyonce-and-jay-z-attendtrayvon-martin-rally-in-nyc.

Hartman, Saidiya. *Lose Your Mother: A Journey Along the Atlantic Slave Route.* New York: Farrar, Straus and Giroux, 2007.

Hastings, Deborah. "Browns' Andrew Hawkins Defends Wearing Tamir Rice T-shirt." *Daily News.* December 16, 2015. Accessed March 25, 2015. www.nydailynews.com/sports/football/andrew-hawkins-defends-decisions-wear-tamirrice-t-shirt-article-1-2047059.

History.com. "Emmet Till." Accessed March 16, 2015. www.history.com/topics/black history/Emmett-till.

History.com. "Stokely Carmichael." Accessed March 19, 2015. www.history.com/topics/blackhistory/stokely-carmichael.

History.com. "Civil Rights Act." Accessed May 8, 2015. http://www.history.com/topics/black-history/civil-rights-act

Howard-Pitney, David. *Martin Luther King, Jr. Malcolm X, and the Civil Rights Struggle of the 1950s and 1960s: A Brief History with Documents.* New York: Bedford/St. Martin Press, 2004.

International Civil Rights Walk of Fame. "Harold George 'Harry' Belafonte, Jr.: 1929- Present." Accessed March 16, 2015. www.nps.gov/features/malu/feat0002/wof/Harold_Belafonte.htm.

It's About Time: Black Panther Party Legacy & Alumni. "The Black Panther Party: Ten Point Platform & Program." October 1966. Accessed March 18, 2015.www.itsabouttimebpp.comn/home/bpp_program_platform.

Joseph, Peniel. "South Africans and African Americans Bound by Struggle." December 8, 2013. *The Root*. Accessed March 17, 2015. www.theroot.com/articles/politics/2013/12/antiapatheid_s_and_civil_rights-special_relationship.

KDrama Stars. "Celebrities Supporting 'Black Lives Matter': Picture of Athletes, Actors & Singers Protesting Police Brutality in the Deaths of Trayvon Martin, Michael Brown, Eric Garner & Tamir Rice." Accessed March 25, 2015. www.kdramastars.com/articles/62034/20141216/celebraities-support-trayvon-martin-michael-brown-eric-garnder-tamir-rice-photo-gallery.

Kehinde Wiley Studio. "Kehinde Wiley." Accessed March 23, 2015. www.kehindewiley.com.

Knowles, David. "Michelle Obama Convinced Husband 'Yes We Can' Slogan Wasn't Corny." Buzzwords. February 16, 2015. Accessed March 25, 2015. www.bloomberg.com/politics/articles/2015-02-16/michelle-obama-convinced-husbandyes-we-can-slogan-wasn-t-corny.

Know Your Meme. "Black Twitter." Accessed March 25, 2015. www.knowyourmeme.com/memes/black-twitter.

Last.fm. "Fugees: Biography." Accessed March 24, 2015. www.last.fm/music/Fugees/+wiki.

Laverne Cox. "Laverne Cox." Accessed March 25, 2015. www.lavernecox.com.

Lewis, Jone Johnson. "National Black Feminist Organization (NBFO). About Education. Accessed March 20, 2015. www.womenshistory.about.com/od/aframorgs/fl/NationalBlack-Feminist-Organization-NBFO.

Lewis, Jone Johnson. "Shirley Chisholm Facts." About Education. Accessed March 20, 2015. www.womenshistory.about.com/od/congress/p/shirleychisholm.

Malcolm X.com. "Biography." Accessed March 14, 2015. www.malcolmx.com.

Malcolm X.com. "Eulogy." Accessed March 14, 2015. www.malcolmx.com.

Martin Luther King, Jr. and the Global Freedom Struggle. Student Nonviolent Coordinating Committee (SNCC). Accessed March 13,2015.

Mascarenhas-Swan, Marc. "Honoring the 44th Anniversary of the Black Panther's Free Breakfast Program." January 18, 2013. Accessed March 18. 2015.www.organizingupgrade.com/index.pp/modules-menu/community-honoring-the-44thanniversary-of-the-black-panthers-free-breakfast-program.

Mitchell, Jerry. "Alabama Jury Convicts Former Klansman." Fold3. Accessed March 16, 2015. www.fold3.com/page/110458149_four_little_girls_the_sixteeenth_street/stories/#21358/.

MLK Online. "Letter from Birmingham Jail." Accessed March 13, 2015. www.mlk.online.net/jail. "Morgan Rhodes." Morgan Rhodes. Accessed March 25, 2015. www.morganrhodes.co.

MSNBC. "Al Sharpton." Accessed March 24, 2015. www.msnbc.com/politicsnation-al-   sharpton/rev-al/sharpton-biography."

Muhammad Ali and Civil Rights." Accessed March 17, 2015. www.aliandcivilrights.weebly.com/the-civil-rights-movement.

Napokoski, Linda. "Combahee River Collective. About Education. Accessed March 20, 2015. www.womenshistory.about.com/od/timeslines19501999/a/combahee_river.

National Archives. "Teaching with Documents: Beyond the Playing Field – Jackie Robinson, Civil Rights Advocate." Accessed March 16, 2015. www.archives.gov/education/lessons/jackie-robinson.

Nation of Islam. "About the Million Man March." Accessed March 23, 2015. www.noi.org/about-million-man-march.

Nelson, Keith. "Questlove Explains Tommy Hilfiger's Comments About 1990s Hip Hop." All HipHop. April 24, 2014. Accessed March 25, 2015. www.allhiphop.com/2014/24/questlove-explains-tommy-hilfigers-comments-about   1990s-hip-hop.

Nobelprize.org. "Dr. Martin Luther King, Jr., Acceptance Speech." Accessed March 13, 2015. www.nobelprize.org/nobel_prizes/peace/laureatees/1964/king-bio.

Nobelprize.org. "Martin Luther King, Jr." Accessed March 13, 2015. www.nobelprize.org/nobel_prizes/peace/laureatees/1964/king-bio.

Nobelprize.org. "Ralph Bunche, Biography." Accessed May 8 2015. http://www.nobelprize.org/nobel_prizes/peace/laureates/1950/bunche-bio.html

Nordquist, Richard. "'I Have a Dream,' by Dr. Martin Luther King, Jr."
     About Education. Accessed March 16, 2015. www.grammar.about.
     com/od/classicessays/a/dreamspeech_2.
NPR. "The Arab Spring: A Year of Revolution." December 11, 2011.
     Accessed March 13, 2015. www.npr.org/2011/12/17/143897126/the-
     arab-spring-a-year-of-revolution. Oprah Winfrey Leadership Acade-
     my for Girls. Accessed March 11, 2015. www.owla.co.za.
Orlousky, Paul. "Tamir Rice Family Calling for 'Direct Indictment."
     19W010. January 6, 2015. Accessed March 25, 2015.
     www.19actionnews.com/19actionnews/pm_/contentdetail.
Patrisse Cullors. "Power from the Mouths of the Occupied."
     Accessed March 25, 2015. www.patrissecullors.com.
PBS.org. "African American World." Accessed March 16, 2015.
     www.pbs.org/wnet/aaworld/timeline/civil_04.
Planer, Lindsay. "Review: John Coltrane. My Favorite Things."
     All Music. Accessed March 11, 2015. www.allmusic.com/album/
     my-favorite-things-mw0000232250.
Poets.org. "Audre Lorde." Accessed March 20, 2015. www.poets.org/
     poetsorg/poet-audre-lorde.
Poets.org. "Nikki Giovanni." Accessed March 19, 2015. www.poets.org/
     poetsorg/poet/nikki-giovanni.
Poets.org. "Sonia Sanchez." Accessed March 20, 2015. www.poets.org/
     poetsorg/poet/sonia-sanchez.
Quora. "Did Malcolm X Speak at the United Nations?" Accessed March 14,
     2015. www.quora.com/Did-Malcolm-X-speak-at-the-united-nations.
Rainbow Push. "Rainbow Push Coalition." Accessed March 24, 2015.
     www.rainbowpush.org.
Ramirez, Ericka. "Grammys 2015: Pharrell Williams, Beyoncé, Prince Pay
     Tribute to Black Lives Matter Movement." Billboard. February 9, 2015.
     Accessed March 25, 2015.www.billboard.com/articles/events/gram-
     mys-2015/6465687/grammys-pharrell-williamsbeyonce-prince-black-
     lives-matter-hands-up-don't-shoot.
Rastafari Speaks Archive 1. "Black Feminism in the US." August 21, 2004.
     Accessed March 20, 2015. www.rastafarispeaks.com/cgi-bin/forum/
     archive1/config.pl?md=read;id=43728.
Renee Cox. "Renee Cox." Accessed March 23, 2015. www.reneecox.
     org/#!about/ciaa.

Revolutionary Worker. "New York: Protests Denounce Police Murder of Amadou Diallo." April 11, 1999. Accessed March 24, 2005. www.revcom.us/a/v20/1000-1009/1001/diallo.

Roman, Christian. "Key Hashtags in 'Black Twitter' Activism. TimesVideo. August 13, 2014. Accessed March 25, 2015. www.nytimes.com/video/us/100000003053125/key-hashtagsin-black-twitter-activism.

Romare Bearden Foundation. "Romare Bearden Biography." Accessed March 23, 2014. www.beardenfoundation.org/artlife/biography/biography.

Rosales, Benn. "Obama Says –Yes We Can, With Social Media & More." The American Genius. November 6, 2008. Accessed March 25, 2015. www.agbeat.com/businessmarketing/obama-says-yes-we-can-with-social-media-more.

Rosenberg, Jennifer. "Muhammad Ali: A Biography of a Famous Boxer." About Education. Accessed March 17, 2015. www.history1900s.about.com/od/people/a/muhammadalo_2.

Rotten Tomatoes. "Selma." Accessed March 23, 2015. www.rottentomatoes.com/m/selma.

RUN-DMC. "RUN DMC." Accessed March 24, 2015. www.rundmc.history.

Rutledge, Pamela. "How Obama Won the Social Media Battle in the 2012 Presidential Campaign." The Media Psychology Blog. January 25, 2013. Accessed March 25, 2015. www.nprcenter.org/blog/2013/01/how-obama-won-the-social-media-battle-in-the-2012presidential-campaign.

Salaam, Kalamu ya. "Historical Overviews of the Black Arts Movement." 1995. Accessed March11, 2015. www.english.illinois.edu.

Senate.gov. Edward Brooke. Accessed May 8, 2015. http://www.senate.gov/artandhistory/history/common/generic/Featured_Bio_Brooke.htm

Simmonds, Yusuf. "Sammy Davis Jr." July 30, 2009. Los Angeles Sentinel. Accessed March 17, 2015. www.lasentinel.net/index.pho?option=com_content&view=article&id=5641:sammy-davis&catid=79&Itemid=169.

Slattery, Denis. "Jay Z, Beyoncé Appear at 'Justice for Trayvon Martin' Vigil in Manhattan with Slain Teen's Mother." Daily News. July 20, 2014. Accessed March 25, 2015. www.nydailynews.com/new-york/jay-z-beyonce-justice-trayvon-martin-vigil-manhattanslain-teen-mother-article-1.1404385.

Smithsonian Folkways. "Voices of the Civil Rights Movement:
    Black American Freedom
Songs 1960-1966." Accessed March 12, 2015. www.folkways.si.edu/
    voices-of-the-civil-rights-movement-black-american-freedom-
    songs-1960-1966/african-american-music-documentary-strug-
    gle-protest/album/Smithsonian.
Smith, Edwin. "Civil Rights Activist Harry Belafonte's Challenge:
    Keep the Movement Alive." Ole Miss. Accessed March 16, 2015.
    www.news.olemiss.edu/civil-rights-activist-harry-belafontes-chal-
    lenge-keep-the-movement-alive-2#.VQeu9Wt5mSM.
SMNTKS. "Black (Celebrity) Lives Matter (More)." January 9, 2015.
    Accessed March 25, 2015.www.smntks.com/2015/01/09/
    black-celebrity-lives-matter-more.
SNCC 1960-1966. "Six Years of the Student Nonviolent Coordinating
    Committee." Accessed March 12, 2015. www.ibiblio.org/sncc/index.
Social Justice Movements. "Angela Davis Biography." Accessed March 19,
    2015. www.socialjustice.ccnmtl.columbia.edu/index.php/
    Angela_Davis_Biography.
Spartacus Educational. "Bobby Seale." Accessed March 19, 2015.
    www.spartacus-educational.com/USAseale.
Spartacus Educational. "Fred Hampton." Accessed March 18, 2015.
    www.spartacus-educational.com/USAhamptonF.
Stableford, Dylan. "Live Updates: Ferguson Protests, Day 10."
    Yahoo. News. Accessed March 23, 2015. www.news.yahoo.com/
    ferguson-protests-live-updates-day-10.
Steptoe, Javaka. "Javaka Steptoe." Accessed March 23, 2015.
    www.javaka.com/index.
"Stokely Carmichael: Black Power Address at UC Berkeley." October 1966.
    American Rhetoric: Top 100 Speeches. Accessed March 18, 2015.
    www.americanrhetoric.com/speeches/stokelycarmichaelblackpower.
Strauss, Chris. "LeBron James, Kyrie Irving and Nets players wear "I Can't
    Breathe' Shirts Before Cavs Game. USA Today Sports. December 8,
    2014. Accessed March 25, 2015. www.ftw.usatoday/2014/12/kyrie-ir-
    ving-i-cant-breathe-t-shirt-before-cavaliers-ericgarner-lebron-james.
Straziuso, Jason. "Nelson Mandela, Martin Luther King Fought the Same
    Battle in Different Continents. Huffington Post Black Voices. August 20,
    2013. Accessed March 17, 2015. www.huffingtonpost.com/2013/08/20/
    nelson-mandela-matin-luther-king_n_37861.

TechTerms.com. "Instagram." Accessed March 25, 2015. www.techterms.
com/definition/instagram.

TechTime.com. "Facebook." Accessed March 25, 2015. www.techterms.
com/defintion/facebook.

The Atlantic. "Martin Luther King's 'Letter
from Birmingham Jail.' April 16, 2013. Accessed March 13, 2015. www.
theatlantic.com/politics/archive/2013/04/martin-luther-kings-letter-
from-Birmingham-jail/274668. The Cleveland Museum of Art. "Hank
Willis Thomas." October 20, 2013. Accessed March 23,2015. www.
clevelandart.org/events/exhibitions/hank-willis-thomas. The Encyclopedia of Arkansas History & Culture. "Little Rock Nine." Accessed
March 16,2015. www.encyclopediaofarkansas.net/encyclopedia//
entry-detail.aspx?entryid=723.

The Famous People. "Huey P. Newton: Biography." Accessed March 19,
2015. www.thefamouspeople.com/profiles/huey-percy-newton-1648.

The History Makers. "Samella Lewis." Accessed March 23, 2015.
www.thehistorymakers.com/biography/samella-lewis

"The Life of Jackie Robinson: Civil Rights Activist." Accessed March 16,
2015. www.solipsis.com/jackierobinson/civil-rights.

"The Official Website of Dr. Maulana Karenga." Accessed March 17, 2015.
www.maulankareng.org.

"The Sculpture of Elizabeth Catlett." Accessed March 23, 2015.
www.elizabethcatlett.net.

The Talking Drum. "Million Youth March." Accessed March 23, 2015.
www.thetalkingdrum.com/mym.

The White House. "President Barack Obama." Accessed March 11, 2015.
www.whitehouse.gov/adminstration/president-obama.

This Day in History. "1968, Dr. King is Assassinated." Accessed March 11,
2014. *www.history.com*/this-day-in-history/dr-king-is-assassinated.

Thurm, Eric. "A Beginner's Guide to Hip-Hop Collective Native Tongues."
A.V. Club. July 5, 2013. Accessed March 24, 2015. www.avclub.com/
article/a-beginners-guide-to-hip-hopcollective-native-ton-99750.

Vox, Lisa. "Timeline of the Civil Rights Movement, 1960-1965. About Education. Accessed March 16, 2015. www.afroamhistory.about.com/od/
civilrightsstruggle1/a/timeline1960.

Walker Art Center. "The Art of Kara Walker." Accessed March 23, 2015.
www.learn.walkerart.org/karawalker/Main/Biography

Weathers, Mary Ann. "An Argument for Black Women's Liberation as a Revolutionary Force."Revolutionary010/07/29/mary-ann-weaForce." Caring Labor: An Archive. July 29, 2010. Accessed March 17, 2015. www.caringlabor.wordpress.com/2010/07/29/mary-ann-weathers-an-argument-for-black-womens-liberation-as-a-revolutionary-force.

West's Encyclopedia of American Law. "Civil Rights Movement." 2005. Accessed March 10, 2015. www.encyclopedia.com/topic/Civil_Rights_Movement.aspx 3/10/15.

Williams, Kam. "Russell Simmons: 'Cops Aren't Indicted Because Police Get to Police Themselves." BlackNews.Com. December 24, 2014. Accessed March 25, 2015. www.blacknews.com/news/russel-simons-cops-arent-indicted-because-police-get-topolice-themselves/#.VRNx22t5mSM.

Women's Tennis Association. "Serena Williams." Accessed March 10, 2015. www.wtatennis.com/players/pplayer/9044.

Wong, Julia. "Trans Activists hold #TurnUp4TransPeople Protest Following Murder of TransWoman. The Daily Dot. February 12, 2015. Accessed March 25, 2015.

World History Archives. "Black Feminist Thought in the Matrix of Domination." AccessedMarch 20, 2015. www.hartford-hwp.com/archives/45a/index-cf.

WuTangCorp.com. "Wu-Tang Clan." Accessed March 23, 2015. www.wutang-corp/artist/wu-tang-clan.

Ya Salaam, Kalamu. "Historical Background of the Black Arts Movement (BAM)." Assata Shakur Forums. Accessed on March 20, 2015. www.assatashakur.org/forum/liberationstrategy/33259-historical-background-black-arts-movement-bam.

Young, Gary. "The Man Who Raised a Black Power Salute at the 1968 Olympic Games." The Guardian. March 30, 2012. Accessed March 17, 2015. www.theguardian.com/world/2012/mar/30/black-power-salute-1968-olympics.

INDEX

CONTINUE THE
CONVERSATION

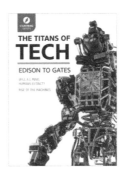
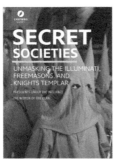

CPSIA information can be obtained at www.ICGtesting.com
Printed in the USA
BVOW11s0208290515

402313BV00002B/2/P